The
of the
Night

MJ CULLINANE

Even a happy life cannot be without a measure of darkness, and the word happy would lose its meaning if it were not balanced by sadness. It is far better take things as they come along with patience and equanimity.

~Carl Jung

The Guardian of the Night Tarot
Copyright © 2020 by MJ Cullinane

Preparing to Use Your Deck

I don't know about you, but when I get a new deck, I am so excited that I just want to jump in and start using it right away. Like a child on Christmas morning, I rip open the box and sift through the cards one by one with delight looking for little hidden images or small details. I look at each image up close and then from a distance to get a feel for its unique energy. Each card holds power and tells a story, and it is in this initial meeting that I connect with all the personalities and their quirks that reside within the deck. Some of the cards create a warm, comforting feeling like that of a good friend, others come off strong and create friction.

I use various methods to clear negative energy that builds up over time on my decks, and that includes first clearing myself of any negative vibes. If I am not in a good space energetically speaking while cleaning my deck, it's like mopping the floor while wearing a big old pair of muddy boots! The shower (aka my portal to the beyond) is a great place to let bad vibes go down the drain. I imagine the water as pure light energy washing away all the murky mucky-muck that tends to build up over time. Another technique and not to go too far down the woo-woo hole here is to imagine that holding all that negative junk in your body is one of those rubber tub stoppers with a metal chain. Imagine it is near your belly button or Solar Plexus. Now envision giving the metal chain a good tug until the rubber stopper comes out, and with it, you release all the emotional toxins that seep into our bodies as a result of just—well—living.

The sun, when present (I am in Seattle, so it's often hit or miss nine-months out of the year), is also an excellent resource for clearing away any negative energy. The power of its light is transformative, and it doesn't take long, nor does it require you to get naked (unless you are into that, and that is awesome too—you and Ben Franklin, in that case, have something in common.)

I find just ten to fifteen minutes sitting comfortably in the sun does a wonderful job of shifting my mood.

Cleaning the house and saging are two activities that, for me, go hand and hand. Not only do these activities make our home pleasant to be in, but it also raises the overall vibration. Saging I have found has a calming quality for both my child and pup Layla, so overall, it's a big win!

To clear a new deck or to clean a deck that has some negative energy build-up, I start by washing the cards. First, you spread the cards all over a table (image side down) and swish them around. Make sure they are nicely mixed up. Then let your intuition guide you around the table, picking up a card from one area then a couple from another. When you have about a third of the cards in your hand, shuffle them until you feel ready to stop and then put that stack aside.

Go back to the table and pick up some more cards from various places until you have only a third remaining. Shuffle the cards and set them next to the first stack. Finally, gather the remaining cards and shuffle those as well. Stack the piles however you like and then shuffle the deck as a whole. If it is a full moon, that evening set the deck near a window that allows the moonlight to come in.

You may also want to keep your deck protected by using crystals such as clear quartz in your deck bag on the box.

Before you touch the deck of cards to do a reading, clear your mind. The goal is to transition into a space of feeling at peace and connected to divine energy. I find floral scents such as jasmine and rose help me escape from day to day stress and create a feeling of inner calm. You may find going for a walk is your path to your higher-self. Sometimes turning up the music and dancing can do wonders for disconnecting from stress. However, it is that you get to a place of peace; it is in the end up to you.

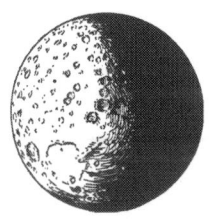

Single Card: Yes / No / Maybe

To use the Guardian of the Night Tarot as an oracle simply think of a question that can be answered as a yes or a no. Shuffle the deck while you focus on your query. When you feel that little tug that lets you know the answer is ready to be revealed, draw your card.

The Fool
The Magician
The Empress
The Chariot
Strength
The Star
The Sun
The World

Ace of Wands	Ace of Cups	Ace of Pentacles
Three of Wands	Two of Cups	Three of Pentacles
Four of Wands	Three of Cups	Nine of Pentacles
Six of Wands	Nine of Cups	Ten of Pentacles
Eight of Wands	Ten of Cups	Page of Pentacles
Page of Wands	Queen of Cups	Knight of Pentacles
Knight of Wands		Queen of Pentacles
Queen of Wands	Ace of Swords	King of Pentacles
King of Wands	Six of Swords	
	Page of Swords	
	Queen of Swords	

The Emperor
The Hierophant
The Hanged Man
Death
The Devil
The Tower
Seven of Wands
Ten of Wands
Five of Cups

Two of Swords	Eight of Swords	Four of Pentacles
Three of Swords	Nine of Swords	Five of Pentacles
Five of Swords	Ten of Swords	Six of Pentacles
Seven of Swords	King of Swords	

The High Priestess
The Lovers
The Hermit
The Wheel of Fortune
Justice
Temperance
The Moon
Judgment

Two of Wands	Eight of Cups	Two of Pentacles
Five of Wands	Page of Cups	Seven of Pentacles
Nine of Wands	Knight of Cups	Eight of Pentacles
Four of Cups	King of Cups	
Six of Cups	Four of Swords	
Seven of Cups	Knight of Swords	

SINGLE CARD: ADVICE

Single card draws can be especially useful for rooting out problem areas or knots that keep your energy from flowing smoothly.

Quiet your mind and hold the deck in your hands firmly. You may have a specific question in mind, or you may want to see what information your guides or higher-self wish to convey to you at the moment. Shuffle the deck until you feel that little tug in your gut—pull a card. Sometimes the message comes across loud and clear, like when you are late putting food in your cat's dish! Other times, the message may come to you in a subtle tone that only begins to make sense after time. Then there are those times when —the message is so undeniable, yet we choose to ignore it.

I noticed with my Crow Tarot deck that the same card would appear over and over, and I believe the cats will be very similar as they too are persistent creatures. When this occurs, it is a message that your guides are trying to get your attention, and clearly, you must be either ignoring them or too much in denial to understand the first two or three times. I suggest making a chart and take note of the cards you pull each day.

I created this spread for the Grimalkin Tarot, however it is my favorite for quick readings regardless of the deck I am using.

Motivation: What is your motivation? What is sparking action?

External Influences: What outside influences are adding friction or support to your situation? What is not in your control?

Obstacle: What is getting in your way? Is it real or is it perceived?

Wisdom: The wisdom the cards bring back to you that will help you reach move in the most beneficial direction.

Questions from the Major Arcana

The Fool
"Are you letting the fears or opinions of others prevent you from taking a leap of faith?"

The Magician
"What is your magic power, and are you using it?"

The High Priestess
"When you tune in to the world around you, what do you see, hear, and feel?"

The Empress
"Are you aware of your position in this world—that you are a creator?

"The Emperor
"Who holds you accountable?"

The Hierophant
"Are your traditions and beliefs a source of strength and inspiration, or do they keep you from expanding your knowledge?"

The Lovers
"Can you give yourself to another without losing who you are?"

The Chariot
"Are you in control of the situation?"

Strength
"Can you face adversity with grace and maybe a bit of humor?"

The Hermit
"Where do you feel most at peace?"

The Wheel of Fortune
"Are you playing roulette with your future, or are you making conscious positive choices?"

Justice
"Are the decisions you make today based on logic and wisdom, or are you letting expectations cloud your judgment?"

The Hanged Man
"Do your plans rely on others to help you move forward, if so, can you see your situation from their perspective?"

Death
"Can you find the beauty you hold within, that part of you that has been with you since birth?"

Temperance
"Where is the line between chaos and harmony meet for you, and can you maintain your balance?"

The Devil
"What tempts you into a situation that may be less than desirable?"

The Tower
"Can you hear the rumble before a situation changes your life for good?"

The Star
"Are you able to see the brightness you have within
—that part of yourself that deserves love and belonging?"

The Moon
"Are you showing off your authenticity, or are you trying to portray your vision of your ideal self?"

The Sun
"Will you allow yourself time to bask in the sun to recharge your spirit?"

Judgment
"Are you being transparent?"

The World
"Are you ready to hold the world in your hands?"

THE FOOL

The wolf chased the rabbit through the woods and on to the ice. Although cracks began to appear under the wolf's feet, it had faith that the ice would hold its weight. The rabbit also had confidence that it's lighter weight and speed would be an advantage as it scurried out of the woods and out to the center of the freshly frozen lake. Both creatures had a goal in mind, and both believed that the ice would not fail them. When I created this card, I wanted to illustrate the full energy of the Fool. Not only does the Fool represent letting go of fear and trusting the Universe, but it also suggests a risk of blind faith. Those standing and watching on the side of the lake could perceive both the wolf and the rabbit as foolish.

Traditionally the Fool is all about acting first and thinking later. It is a card that can represent a great adventure as you let go of expectations and proceed on a journey knowing regardless of the outcome, something of value will be gained. When I see this card, the first question that comes to mind is, am I overthinking my next move? The Fool asks that you let go of the need to control every aspect of a situation. Allow events to unfold, and if something appears different than how you expected, perhaps it will turn out to be a pleasant twist as you make your way on a new endeavor?

Animal Keywords:

Wolf: Family, reliance, hope, teamwork, confidence
Rabbit: Abundance, reproduction, open, creativity, luck

THE MAGICIAN

When it came time to create the illustration for the energy of the Magician, the raccoon came forward very strongly, and I knew this was the creature who embodies the traits of the Magician. The raccoon moves through the night swiftly and often undetected, but passive animals they are not! Raccoons are resourceful hunters who understand how to use their resources to their fullest. Whether it is climbing a tree for an egg in a nest or unlatching a neighbor's chicken coop, they will act with passion and determination to get what they desire.

The Magician energy is one that requires action; it requires work. Like casting a spell, preparation and commitment are required. When the Magician appears, you are asked to take control of the situation to make clear and conscious decisions that will open the door for the right opportunity that will, in turn, yield the results you desire. When you pull this card, take a moment to draw in its energy, I find its electricity travels through my hand and into my soul. It is in this moment of connection that you, too, will find a refreshed sense of enthusiasm, of passion, and as a result, you will feel as though you hold the power of the world in your hands.

Animal Keywords:
Raccoon: Nimble, focused, clever, dexterity, determination, passion

THE HIGH PRIESTESS

Can you imagine being a bat, hanging there in the night air, taking it all in without feeling a need to impulsively act on every breeze that brushes by your head? Using all your senses to their fullest? Your long slick wings wrapping around your body as if to make a peaceful cocoon that camouflages you in the trees? There was no other creature I could think of that represents the energy of the High Priestess more than the bat as it is, after all, considered the Guardian of the Night.

The High Priestess travels through the darkness across the veil in silence as she uses her intuition to hone in on the information that will best support you at this time. In return, you must meet her energy using the same frequency for there to be a connection and for her wisdom to be received. This is not a time for impulsive action or telling the world your plans. You will benefit at this time by staying quiet, tuning into your surroundings, and connecting with your intuition.

Although it is in our isolation, in that space where we find quiet, the answers we seek become known, the bat energy is also one of community and serves as a reminder that although there may be times that require solitude or secrecy, we all benefit from being part of something greater than ourselves.

Animal Keywords:
Bat: Magical, intuitive, quiet, esoteric, success, prosperity

THE EMPRESS

The Empress represents motherly love and compassion. It is the energy that nurtures every aspect of your life, from emotional to material. The Empress's power creates an atmosphere conducive for growth and protects you from misfortune. When this card appears, you are being guided and watched over; there is a soothing element present that wants nothing more than to see her child succeed.

You may also want to consider if you are being asked to step into the Empress's role, as someone near may need your love and support to flourish. Experience the world through the eyes of royalty, see the abundance that is yours to enjoy. Because the Empress does not know lack, or a need to compete, her heart is open, and compassion comes naturally. When you walk in the Empress's path, you will have the resources to use your position and privilege to help others.

The mother fox came to mind when illustrating the Empress. I imagined this beautiful vibrant animal protecting her young as it rests underground, connected to Mother-Earth, growing stronger, and shielded from threats. The fox is not only attractive, but she is also innovative and resourceful, and much like the Empress, the fox understands its position and surroundings with complete clarity. The energy of the fox and Empress combined is one of refinement and cunning. It is an energy that creates a strong awareness of all aspects of a situation so that when you proceed, there is an air of protection around you.

Animal Keywords:
Fox: Cleverness, spry, magical, shape shifting

THE EMPEROR

The Emperor can be an intimidating fellow, especially if you have been cutting corners or not giving a situation your full attention. He will hold you accountable for your actions. But he is also a fair ruler, and if you find yourself on the right side of an argument, disagreement, or legal battle, rest assured justice will be served in your favor. Like the Empress, the Emperor's energy may materialize as a signal that it is your time to step up and take on a noble leader's role. Your input or contribution may be needed to solve a problem or mediate a disagreement, ensuring that both parties feel heard and understood.

Noble, healthy, and wise, the Great horned owl came right to mind without hesitation or second-guessing when creating this card. This bird is fierce and possesses a powerful presence, much like how I imagine an Emperor. An interesting fact I learned while researching the animals for this deck, although the Great horned owl goes for traditional owl food such as rodents and frogs, it also hunts more massive creatures, including other birds of prey such as falcons. Also, with talons that close with commanding force that are near impossible for any prey to open and escape, much like an Emperor, the great horned owl's decision is final. This owl offers its courage and wisdom to you if you need to confront a situation or go on the attack. Sometimes a problem requires a level of aggression that demonstrates your command, desire, or passion for a positive outcome. Use this energy wisely and judiciously.

Animal Keywords:
Owl: Wisdom, protection, authority, awareness, guidance

THE HIEROPHANT

When I announced this project's creation, there were quite a few requests for rats to be included. Although I'm a bit squeamish when it comes to this animal, especially after a rental house infestation we experienced when my daughter was baby, nonetheless, I recognize as an animal their contribution and the gifts of wisdom they offer.

The Hierophant energy is tied to our heritage, our culture, and what is expected of us for no other reason other than the "box" we have been put in as a result of our birth. For many, this energy creates acceptance as we connect with others of a familiar vein. It is the Hierophant that shows us the well-worn path that our ancestors have traveled. The Hierophant's energy carries with it the wisdom of the ages, and when the time comes, it will be the teacher you need. Modern or adaptive the Hierophant is not; its energy is traditional and serves to show you how you fit in a box. For some, this is a very comforting place. For others, it can feel stifling. Use the energy of the Hierophant to understand your position, to gain wisdom and knowledge of the past, to find support in a group that feels right. Still, if you are looking for a change or a new perspective, the Hierophant may find your defiance challenging.

When my daughter was little, well younger than today, she loved the movie Ratatouille; frankly, I still find that movie a bit difficult to watch. When illustrating this card, I thought about how the young rat wanted to be a chef, but it faced expectations from all around because it was born a rat. His father expected him to raid kitchens, the cooks expected him to be a dirty thief. The rat was placed in a "box" put there for no other reason than because it was born a rat, it was all the outside world could see.

However, the little rat knew enough about himself to not allow the expectations of others to determine his fate. The rat brings an energy of adaptability; one focuses on problem-solving. When you combine the Hierophant with the rat, you will not only know where you have been but also know where you are going.

Animal Keywords:
Rat: Intelligence, tradition, success, tenacity

THE LOVERS

I started the Guardian of the Night just as school closed for the year due to the coronavirus. During this time, I was hyper-vigilant in making sure the only TV shows during the "school day" were nature or educational programming. That is where I discovered the awesomeness that is the scorpion. Not only does their mating ritual begin with a dance, but some females are also particularly critical of their dancing partner and will cut the night short by killing their date. This is one creature who knows what they like and don't like and isn't afraid of expressing themselves! Scorpions are independent and are self-reliant. They also bring passion and danger to a relationship! Scorpions have a strong intuition, and being so close to the ground, they are firmly centered. When entering a relationship, call upon this wise arachnid to help you create a lasting and mutually fulfilling spark.

Traditionally, the Lovers represents a union of two forces, a relationship that creates strength and passion when forged. However, you are not asked to release your beliefs or conform to another's preferences completely.

Harmony is achieved when the Lovers work together when they allow some give and take to pull out the best from one another. Much like a dance! Whereas the Hierophant represents collective beliefs, the Lover's speaks to your individuality; what ideas and convictions do you offer the relationship? Where is your passion?

Animal Symbolism:
Scorpion: Protection, beliefs, passion, strong opinions
Luna Moth: Rebirth, renewal, change, soul

THE CHARIOT

Do you remember all those Honey Badger memes going around? When it came time to create the Chariot, those memes came to my mind instantly. The honey badger doesn't quit, it takes what it wants, and it does so without giving a damn! The honey badger brings an energy that is of brute force, of pure determination. The honey badger rushes in without a single care in the world, and right now, you might benefit from adding a little of its energy to your situation. Have courage, build up the drive to move forward without over-analyzing the situation. Of course, this energy comes with a caveat, you need to understand how to reign it in, how to harness that power so that it doesn't lead you on a collision course caused by making rash or impulsive decisions.

The honey badger's powerful energy comes forward to help you develop your confidence, ignite passion, and drive. You will find when the honey badger is near, your ability to understand what needs to be done becomes much more evident as the impulse to act grows stronger. Independence grows, you are self-reliant and capable of any challenge that may come your way.

Animal Keywords:
Honey Badger: Grit, focus, independence, healing

STRENGTH

Strength can refer to how physically strong you are, however, in this case strength represents physical restraint and your ability to control your emotions.

The mouse resists the urge to scurry away in the face of danger. The snake resists the urge to indulge in a mid-morning snack. Because of their ability to let go and face their fears, the snake and the mouse can see each other, truly seeing each other as another creature put on this planet with hopes and dreams. It is in this moment of controlling their instincts that the world opens up, and new information can be gained.

If you see yourself as the mouse, you may be feeling as though you are the victim or the prey in your situation, that your needs are dependent on the approval of others. If you perceive your position as one that is at a disadvantage in a situation, for example, you are dealing with a boss or someone in power, call on the mouse's strengths, such as its connection to the earth as it will bring grounding to your situation. Mice are also adaptable and can get through obstacles quickly. If you immediately connected with the snake, you may be feeling as though you are the one that must alter or make concessions, and that can breed resentment. Use this opportunity to grow, to learn from others. You are in a position to create an atmosphere of healing and harmony. Think about how a snake sheds its skin; your current situation may be one that represents a significant time for growth.

Animal Keywords:

Snake: Change, growth, connected, spiritual, flexible, intuition
Mouse: Expressive, resourceful, playful

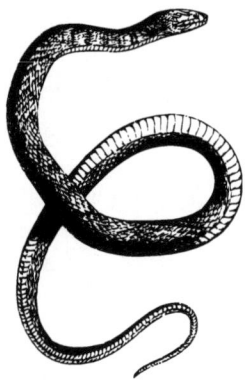

THE HERMIT

Ah, the Hermit, like my other decks, was the first card I created for the Guardian of the Night. This only makes sense since this is usually the energy swirling around as anxiety and uncertainty come together to brew change. In mid-March, when Seattle Public Schools announced that schools were going to be closed for an undetermined amount of time and all of the city was virtually in lock-down, the Hermit emerged to help me ease into a new normal of staying away from others, of staying in and being alone with my thoughts.

The image of a spider weaving a web that not only protects but also provides nourishment came right to mind as my daughter and I, like so many others, found ourselves stocking up and essentially "nesting." Tapping into the energy of the Hermit helped me find the opportunities for wisdom being on lock-down offered. Time spent indoors and not socializing made way for new ideas to flourish and the time to work on them!

The Hermit asks that you seek solitude, find that quiet space that welcomes insight from your higher-self. The Hermit energy is often lost on those who mistake being alone for loneliness or are uncomfortable sitting with only their inner-thoughts. When this card appears, take time and practice the skill of achieving peace while in solitude. Once your mind is in a state of quiet, listen to that faint voice that comes through. Can you hear the guidance?

The spider makes for an ideal Hermit as it is a less-than social creature preferring to spend its time in the shadows. Known for being mysterious, channel this creature when it is time to assess your growth.

Are there opportunities to cast a new net or spin a new web to help you gain the desired outcome? Like the spider, have patience if the results don't happen overnight and pay attention to the vibrations as they will become your guide.

Animal Keywords:
Spider: Patience, creativity awareness, vibration, connected

THE WHEEL OF FORTUNE

Often a sign that things are shifting towards a more positive direction and that your luck is about to change for the better when The Wheel of Fortune makes an appearance, take note! This card is a signal to direct your energy on focusing on what you want to achieve. Can you see the big picture? Forces from above are coming together to help you and will be looking for your direction. What action can you take today to get things rolling? If you need to pivot, now is the time to expand your horizons or see your situation from a new perspective. I have to confess that I get that little flurry of excitement in my belly when I see the Wheel of Fortune, especially if I have been managing a less-than-pleasant situation!

The owls, bats, spiders circle in the night sky to create a vortex of healing, transformative energy. The owls create clarity and the ability to see your goal even in the darkest of nights. The bats bring intuition and make a connection with your higher-self, and the snake at the center is here to help you release the past, shed what no longer serves so that your dreams can grow bigger. Two scorpions and two lunar moths guard the perimeter, ensuring that you remain true to yourself and your values to who you are at the soul level during this change.

Animal Keywords:

Owl: Wisdom, protection, authority, awareness, guidance
Bat: Magical, intuitive, quiet, esoteric, success, prosperity
Snake: Change, growth, connected, spiritual, flexible, intuition
Scorpion: Protection, beliefs, passion, strong opinions
Luna Moth: Rebirth, renewal, change, soul

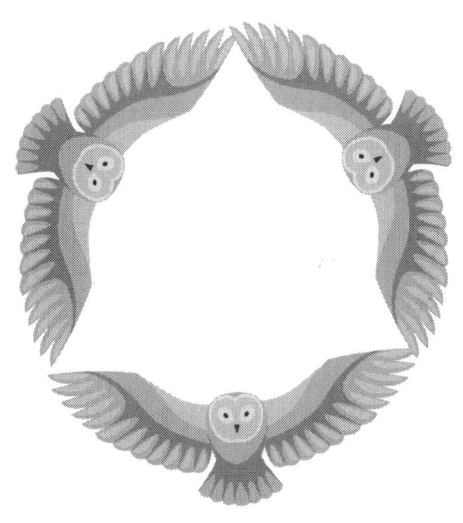

JUSTICE

The Karma card, Justice is blind (although contrary to popular belief, bats are not!), and your actions will have consequences even if they don't materialize right away. When Justice appears, make time to carefully weigh all factors before committing to a final decision. Can you predict the outcome or get a vague impression of what may result? You may not be able to gain a clear vision of what the future will hold, but if you strike a balance between logic and your internal compass, you will tune in to your surroundings and get a feeling for what to expect. Justice will hold you accountable, and if your actions and intentions are out of alignment, if you avoid being truthful with yourself or with others, you feel its swift unwavering ruling.

Like the bat soaring across the night sky using echolocation hunting for a meal through the dark, using only the resources it has at its disposal; you, too, are asked to let your learned knowledge and intuition lead you to an ideal outcome. When you need to make a decision or take action without having all the information laid out neatly in front of you, call upon the energy of the bat for courage as it will guide you as these mystical and magical creatures are in tune with the vibrations of the Universe.

Animal Keywords:
Bat: Magical, intuitive, quiet, esoteric, success, prosperity

THE HANGED MAN

Although it is only after we relax into the fact that we have become immobilized, do the gifts of the Hanged Man become clear. Having the ability to see your situation from a different angle, a new perspective will open the door for other options and, with it new opportunities. In this state of suspension, our creative mind takes in the world from a new angle, and with that imagery, further information is gathered, and ideas emerge. With more information, the opinions that we once held on to so tightly evolve, while some may wither, others will blossom.

The Hanged Man represents inaction, or stagnation at someone's hands or a situation out of our control. This could be as annoying as being put in perma-hold as you are trying to connect with customer service or maybe having a project delayed because the person who needs to sign off on the next step is out on an unexpected medical leave. There is nothing you can do. Although frustrating, the Hanged Man arrives to teach us a fundamental lesson, patience, and the bonus lesson of compassion if your derailment results from someone else's misfortune.

Opossums are not the fighting type; when threatened, they pause all action and play dead. When you are in a momentary limbo state, take a cue from the Opossum and lay low. Fighting during this time will not yield positive results; what it will do is draw attention to perhaps at the worst, you be unprepared for a battle to at the least less than desirable behavior that may create further delays.

Animal Keywords:
Opossum: Passive, perspective, going inward, inaction

DEATH

Many people recoil when the Death card appears in a reading as if it were an omen soon to come, suggesting a passing from this world. Rarely does this card indicate an upcoming loss of life; however, it can very well suggest that life as you know it may be due for a shift. It is time to close a chapter, move on, and let go of something that has run its course. Change, after all, like death, is inevitable. When the Death card appears, you may need to consider if you are devoting too much time and energy to something that no longer offers the growth potential. Much like religiously watering a dead tree, there isn't much you can do to bring it back, and your efforts, although in earnest, will be wasted. You are asked to release yourself from the attachments that no longer offer growth opportunities because, in doing so, will you open the door for something new.

When it came time to illustrate the Death card, I thought about how at times, we do everything in our power to avoid the thing we fear most. For many of us, that is letting go of a limiting belief, getting out of our comfort zone, and embracing a significant life change. Change requires vulnerability, and staying put, or avoidance can be so much easier. However, as time moves on, we continue to grow even in small ways, and that space where we sought refuge remains the same. Eventually, that stagnant space gets tighter, and pricks of discomfort become more noticeable and potentially destructive. In the end, we become painfully stuck. A vision of a low thorn bush and a family of rats seeking safety from an owl appeared in my mind. Fear kept the rats from moving, from using their creative minds—from living. As time went on, the thorn bush encapsulated them and became their cage.

Although they tried to avoid discomfort, their lives in the end still changed, but not for the better. Change is inevitable. The beliefs they nurtured and invested so much time and energy in keeping them in the thorn bush, and when those beliefs no longer served them, they could not see that eventually, those same thoughts lead to their demise.

The owl offers you its wisdom and a sharp sight to identify areas that need to be released. You have the strength to rise up and out of a situation that may be holding you down. Rats are known for their adaptability. When you call on the rat to assist you during a time of flux, you will find within you a natural ability to accept and adjust to a new environment.

Animal Keywords:
Owl: Wisdom, protection, authority, awareness, guidance
Rat: Intelligence, tradition, success, tenacity

TEMPERANCE

Temperance brings a gentle flow of energy to a situation as it creates space for energies to come together and combine without friction. When in Temperance, you can understand the many sides of a problem without feeling dragged down or overwhelmed. Temperance is a space of complete and total control over your emotions and actions. You may have an overflowing to-do list with new tasks added daily, with a myriad of personalities and egos bombarding you and challenging your sanity. Coming at you from left and right, situations are demanding your attention, and yet somehow, you have managed to stay on top of it all and unfrazzled. You are taking it all in stride, not letting things slip by or go unfinished.

You are checking off your to-do list and getting things done while staying as cool a cucumber. When this energy is present, you will find yourself enjoying that golden space of harmony where work and leisure blend together in effortless perfection. It is all about moderation and striking a balance of feeling connected and in control of your emotions. Suppose you have been dealing with a difficult or emotional situation. In that case,

Temperance may arrive as a warning and indicates that a move to the middle away from an extreme or rigid position will prove beneficial. You may need to consider if you are too emotionally invested? If there is a legal matter at hand, a negotiation where common ground is established will benefit both parties. Depending on the situation and the position where Temperance sits, you may hold power to assist a situation by taking on the mediator's role. Your unique perspective and insight will help bring two parties together to reach an amicable outcome. The frog embodies the energy of Temperance as it balances its life in and out of water.

Animal Keywords:
Frog: Growth, balance, prosperity, transformation, good-fortune

THE DEVIL

When we choose to sit on the couch and binge-watch an entire season of a TV show while eating a pint of ice cream, instead of tackling a nagging chore that needs to be done, that is the energy of the Devil testing you, creating an opportunity that feeds your desire for comfort. The Devil brings indulgence, succumbing to slothfulness, and choosing that thing that satisfies our immediate needs instead of facing a challenge. Resisting the Devil can be daunting, to say the least. We often don't recognize it until it is too late, as this crafty creature disguises itself as something intriguing or desirable. One weekend of being an over-indulgent couch potato is something everyone needs every once in a while. However, when it slips into becoming a daily habit, an unhealthy addiction forms, and breaking it will be far more complicated than that original chore. The Devil is cunning, an astute researcher of human nature, its power resides in understanding our weaknesses, as it knows which strings, when pulled, will have the greatest and most destructive effect.

When we choose silence over speaking up, when we play small out of fear of being ridiculed, that is the Devil's work. The energy slips in to create a seed of self-doubt and then reinforces it by feeding ideas for a much more appealing scenario, one that doesn't cause pain. When we refuse to face reality, when we allow ourselves to stay put in a destructive pattern or habit, when the pain or suffering required for freedom is too extreme, we are at the Devil's mercy. This creature finds delight and strengthens when we fall victim to our worst character flaws. When the Devil appears, you may need to examine if something masks itself as an easy solution or a less than challenging alternative.

Animal Keywords:

Jackalope: Myth, legend, man-made, mystical

THE TOWER

The energy can seize our lives in a variety of ways. It could be losing your job, a sudden and unexpected loss of residence, a bill that comes out of the blue that wipes out your savings. The Tower brings swift change that shakes up life as we know it. All the structures we have grown accustomed to, the security that we perhaps have taken for granted, are ripped right from under us, and the feeling of being flung into the air takes over. When the Tower appears in a reading, it may speak to a significant moment in your past that caused a major disruption and, as a result, left you picking up the pieces. It may also arrive as a warning, a sign that something important in your life is about to change. Much like the train's rumbling before it arrives at the station, heed this warning as the train is on the tracks and will come on schedule. The message here is to be prepared. Tap into your intuition. You may already have an idea that changes at work are on the way or that your once rosey relationship is withering. You may have picked up the vibe that your landlord is planning to sell the building; whatever it is, the Tower can be a gift as it will allow you to plan your next move. Because vultures need warm thermal updrafts, they are unable to fly at night. I thought about how these communal creatures, these big, bold, and during the day, intimidating birds, would be thrown into a state of panic if they were suddenly tossed out of their nightly nest. I imagined that initial state of frenzy; it is the same sensation that we humans feel when the foundation we have become so accustomed to is ripped right from under us. The Vulture, however, is no pushover, it doesn't cower or fall prey to disaster; on the contrary, it is a fighter and scavenger. This creature finds opportunities in a death and brings you the strength to rise up through the dust into the sun's warmth.

Animal Keywords:

Vulture: Community, harmony, restoration

The Star

When I think of the Star's energy, the word grace comes to mind and of being at peace with oneself and the world. There is a quiet confidence woven within this card that brings to a situation a firm knowing that everything will be okay even when confronting the most challenging struggle. When you open your heart to the Star, when you allow its vibrant bright light to wash away any self-doubt, any negative feelings that once kept you pinned down will release. A new sense of empowerment will instill within a feeling of being nimble and capable of overcoming any obstacle. Call on the deer to help you connect with the energy of the Star as this sensitive yet strong creature with its heightened senses establishes a feeling within of being connected to the planet, of being in tune with your surroundings. When you are given the Star's gift, lean into its illuminating presence, and a feeling of confidence will be restored.

Animal Keywords:
Deer: Intuition, confidence, protection

THE MOON

Around the same time, I was working on the Major Arcana for the Guardian of the Night, coyote sightings in our neighborhood within Seattle seemed to be at an all-time high. Of course, there were many people sympathetic to this creature's forced evolution into urban wildlife. In contrast, others panicked at the thought of our city streets becoming hunting grounds for hungry coyotes. My mind went to the coyote, not seeing or believing its surroundings had changed, that it remained in the wild and, as a result, went about life just as it would if all the townhomes, apodments, and fancy new restaurants were not there. Of course, the recent influx of easy food was something the coyote merely enjoyed but didn't ponder over too much. The Moon appears when the time has come for you to see a situation for how it is in reality not how you prefer it to appear.

You are asked to dive deep into the darkness of your subconscious and explore what dwells within. Use your imagination to examine your fears and anxieties and explore freely, giving the unknown space to come out from the shadows. Do you see your life as it is in reality, or are you constructing a story that feels more comfortable and familiar? Call upon the cunning and quick-witted coyote when you must face a complicated reality as this trickster to help you see the humor and the lighter side of life.

Animal Keywords:
Coyote: Trickery, adaption, cleverness, hiding in the shadows

THE SUN

Although some illustrations for this deck took some time to visualize before getting to work on creating the art, the Sun was not one of them. This card came through almost instantly. I could see the tree with the mountain lion, I could see the valley in the distance and the sun as it crested the horizon line with complete clarity. Knowing what the illustration should look like takes a significant amount of time, and with this one, it was illuminated entirely, like the Sun.

When the Sun appears in a reading, be prepared to be seen for your talents to be recognized and for your efforts to be acknowledged. You will feel a warm energy take over as those around you express admiration and support. The mighty Sun also helps you see something that will benefit your situation; something new that would typically be overlooked will shine and stand out so that you don't miss it. When you bask in the sun's light, you will feel bold and confident, you will have an urge to stand up to be seen. You are asked to trust that your abilities and talents will open the door to new opportunities. However, be aware that the Sun shines bright, and if you are operating with less than noble intentions, those too will be in the light. Mountain Lions/cougars walk this planet with a knowing that they are sacred and command the attention of all who pass in their presence. They possess no need to tell the world of their greatness; they only need to stare at you from a tree limb to see it in your face. Call upon the authentic and powerful energy of the Mountain Lion when you need that added boost of confidence, and you too will feel as though you are the ruler of the forest.

Animal Keywords:
Mountain Lion: Authentic, strength, confidence, generous

JUDGMENT

Like the Sun, the illustration for Judgment came right away. I visited a friend who has a little lake house on the Olympic Peninsula and came across a snakeskin during one of our walks. Like a bolt to the brain, the image of the Judgment card hit me. Of course, what better animal to represent shedding the past and transformation than a snake!

Judgment indicates a notable turning point and calls on you to examine your life as a whole, the good, the bad, and yes, even the ugly. When this card appears, we are encouraged to open up and be honest, to not make excuses for our failures, or point fingers at those who negatively impacted our lives. The time has come to shed the past, own up to our own actions and contributions, and take responsibility to spark growth.

When you accept yourself fully, your situation will benefit as this is time for significant development.When you call upon the snake's energy, you will find support during a time of transformation. The snake is also a symbol of healing, using its power to help you release painful moments from the past to grow all the stronger in the future.

Animal Keywords:
Snake: Change, growth, connected, spiritual, flexible, intuition

THE WORLD

You know that feeling you get after the last dinner guest leaves after an epic evening of great food and conversation. You're stuffed, exhausted, and exhilarated at the same time. That is the feeling The World brings to your situation. It is an energy of complete and utter satisfaction. Not only did something end on a positive note, but you are also left feeling grateful and in love with life. A long journey has come to an end, a victorious end, and although yes, there are new experiences to be had, for now, you are given permission to simply bask in the joy that comes from a much-earned success.

When I created this card, I wanted everyone to feel when holding it a celebration of life and excitability that comes from the hope for a brighter future.

Call upon the bee's busy, productive energy to help you reach that ending you desire as this small but mighty creature can help you taste the sweetness of success. On the bottom of this card, you will find a grasshopper to represent the abundance and prosperity you will achieve from your efforts. The grasshopper is also a symbol of being true to yourself, living your life, not imitating others as your life is about to take a leap forward.

Animal Keywords:
Bee: Collaboration, community, prosperity, sweetness of life
Grasshopper: Prosperity, good fortune, abundance

ACE OF WANDS

A new adventure awaits! The Ace of Wands brings forward an original path, a new reason to feel enthusiastic about a blossoming situation. This is not the time to sit back and wait for things to happen; no, now is the time to let your creative mind explore all the possibilities.

When the Ace of Wands appears, you will benefit significantly from mustering up the courage and letting yourself entertain new and imaginative ideas. This is not the time for self-doubt or second-guessing. Pay attention to your gut and areas that call your attention. Like a spider's web, you will feel the vibration when something of value is near. Pay attention to the signs and follow your gut as it will lead you down a path to fresh opportunities.

Call upon the firefly's energy when you need to feel comforted in the dark or when you need the courage to move forward without knowing exactly where you are going. This small creature illuminates the darkest of nights. When you use its energy, you will feel a brightness glowing from within, which will help guide you as you move forward. The spider lends its energy by offering creativity and sensitivity to vibration. The spider knows how to craft the perfect web, one that will yield the greatest return without being caught up in itself. Although a new adventure is forming, the spider also brings restraint. Having the ability to create a foundation for success is but one part of the equation; the spider also possesses patience knowing in time its hard work will pay off and it will attract its desired outcome.

Animal Keywords:

Spider: Patience, creativity awareness, vibration, connected

Fire Fly: Guidance, creativity, inspiration

Two of Wands

The story I created in my mind for the Two of Wands was one of a lioness who was tired of her mate swooping in at the last minute after she did all the hard work of taking down dinner and wanted the rewards for herself. While the male lion lounged around the plain, the lioness concocted a plan that, if successful, would not only gain a reputation of a fierce leader, she would also enjoy the lion's share of the kill.

The Two of Wands indicates that it is time to take a bold move or risk that you may have shied away from in the past. When you approach a situation with confidence, sharing your vision for the future as a pioneer will support you. This is not a time to fall back on the tried and true, or play it safe; no, this is a time to be original and step forward to claim your personal power. Resist the urge to second-guess your decision. If you spent time considering all angles, consulted with those who may feel the impact, and weighed in all the information available to you, let it go and be final. If you are concerned about the outcome and can see the possibility of regret in the future, there is also no shame in holding off on making a decision; just do so with clarity and conviction.

When you need the confidence to make a decision, especially one that puts you outside the status-quo, call upon the lion's nurturing feminine energy for protection. Let this regal and graceful animal guide you into a state of confidence as you break free from the pack.

Animal Keywords:
Lion: Passion, command, authority, royalty, power, prestige

THREE OF WANDS

Your current situation may benefit from broadening your horizons by looking beyond the present to what could be in the future. There is a great big world out there waiting to be explored! The Three of Wands asks that you not jump into action without a plan. You have plenty of time to get the details right, and when you focus your energy on creating a vision for where you want to go, a road map will appear.

The Three of Wands is a green light to get off the fence and take action. Go forward, knowing that where you end up will be a positive place. When thinking about the message of the Three of Wands, I thought about birds that migrate.

The Scissor-Tailed Flycatcher moves through the dark skies as it returns from Central America to North America's plains. What I find interesting, aside from that, they can navigate their way through the night for thousands of miles. They tend to wander, perhaps not settling for what is closest but rather an area that feels right. Call on this beautiful songbird when you need to get that traveling itch as this bird is not afraid of putting in the miles.

Animal Keywords:
Scissor-Tailed Flycatcher: Migration, path, expansion, travel

FOUR OF WANDS

The noisy raucous magpie called out loudly as if there was any other way to represent the joyful Four of Wands. You are being offered the gift of a potent dose of positive energy. Lean wholeheartedly into the Four of Wands's energy. Can you feel that excitement swirling around as a celebration is approaching?

When you embrace a party spirit, you create a frequency that will open the door for an encounter with someone who will play a pivotal role in helping you achieve a desire. This person may end up being your next romantic relationship; they may have a connection to your dream job or future business partner. The key will be to let go of expectations and simply enjoy the party, let go of any material desires and live in the moment as that is how you will tune in and attract the opportunity.

Having a hard time getting pumped for the party? Call upon the talkative Magpie's energy for balance as this flirty bird will give you the courage to strike up a conversation with just about anybody.

Animal Keywords:
Magpie: Communication, creativity, community, fun, playfulness

Five of Wands

You know those days when you wake with a plan only to throw it in the garbage because apparently, the Universe didn't get the memo. Your day is spent putting out fires, dealing with things that seem to have popped up out of nowhere, and just as you think you have everything done, something else arises to steal you away. You may experience one of those days that leaves you feeling as though every person you encounter has a different opinion, and no one can seem to agree.

The Five of Wands implies that you will discover some drama due to petty debates, demands, or just life. If you are one to look on the bright side, this may be an excellent opportunity to get some outside perspective or slow down. The idea of a beaver working tirelessly to create a home while contending with the rough waters came into mind when making the Five of Wands. I just thought about this poor creature being at the mercy of something so overpowering and uncontrollable, yet at the same time, unfettered and focused on staying on task.

The beaver is a wise master builder who offers us the wisdom of constructing boundaries that will ensure that we stay on task. Like the dams they build, you may need to slow down a bit, practice a little restraint, and not let every impulse or desire to act break through.

Animal Keywords:
Beaver: Construction, boundaries, determination, creativity, having fortitude

Six of Wands

Victory is yours! Take it all in as you become wrapped in the warm graces of those who appreciate your dedication and hard work. Savor the praise while you receive it and then continue building upon your success. The Six of Wands calls on you to allow yourself the pleasure of basking in the glory of your success. When you take a moment to celebrate your achievements, your self-esteem will get a boost, and in return, you will feel invincible. Ride this sensation as it will create a ripple effect that will help propel you forward but do not rely on the past to guarantee future successes. As with any victory, it is merely a stepping stone.The Six of Wands may also indicate an opportunity to be an inspiring leader. Your success will open the door for you to not only realize your full potential; you also will have the ability to assist others as they embark on their journey. When you see yourself as a contributor to the greater good, not only will you help or inspire others to reach for their goals, you will solidify your success.

You may come to think of his card as I do, as the King Julian card for those of you who have kids. Ah, that highly extroverted and, at times, pompous lemur king from Madagascar. The lemur is a highly social creature and offers an energy that is agile and full of fun; these Madagascan tree-dwellers understand the value of community and know how to enjoy life's simple pleasures. Call upon the lemur if you feel uneasy being the center of attention or accepting praise as it will help you find the confidence to proudly take ownership of your successes.

Animal Symbolism:
Lemur: Extroverted, Playful, confident, community

Seven of Wands

The Seven of Wands speaks to holding your position, of digging in your heels and not giving an inch. You may feel like an alligator, low to the ground, concrete, and connected to your beliefs; use this to your benefit if you encounter someone who challenges your philosophy.

The Seven of Wands may also point to those around you who feel threatened by your position or who may feel a need to challenge you. If you know you are in the right, hold firm. When you commit to your place, you will be unshakable. Others around you may not be able to see the whole picture from their vantage point and will be at a disadvantage as you can see a situation from a better perspective. The Seven of Wands may also point to a time of feeling under attack, of feeling as though everyone is strategizing against you.

Are you overly defensive and, as a result, the one who is looking for a fight? Are you holding on to a shoreline when it would be more beneficial to get in the water? Call upon the spirit of the alligator to help you connect with Mother-Earth and grounding. This animal knows how to thrive both in and out of the water and can help you find that balance between your emotions and logical mind. Although heavy, it can also teach us buoyancy as we ride down the river of life.

Animal Keywords:
Alligator: Mental stability, grounded, harmony, sharpness, creation, fresh start

EIGHT OF WANDS

When thinking about the Eight of Wands message, I thought about how birds hundreds of feet in the air see their prey. How they envision a successful conclusion before diving at record speeds towards earth to pluck up their meal. They commit to the action, they release any fear, and with complete control, they execute a plan. The Eight of Wands is a card of envisioning success, of taking swift undeniable action, and moving forward without pause or second-guessing yourself. The energy housed in this card is vibrant; however, it can be a bit volatile, and as a result, you need to move swiftly and allow room for change; you need to be agile and flexible; otherwise, you will lose momentum. Just as the falcon is prepared for its prey to move, you too may need to adjust your course. To avoid friction or conflict, release any need for rigid planning and let go of any expectations; this will allow you to adapt or modify plans easily. You will find ideas and situations will progress quickly when the Eight of Wands is present—keep your eyes open as you may miss valuable information as a result of pushing ahead so quickly.

Call upon the falcon when you need to get a broad view of your situation as this bird can find opportunities over a wide area. Not only will you benefit from this bird's keen vision, it's ability to master the wind will help you maintain a steady pace regardless of obstacles that may try to blow you off course. The falcon is also a messenger and may bring valuable news to help you during a trying situation.

Animal Keywords:
Falcon: Control, patience, precision, speed, adaptable

NINE OF WANDS

The word that comes to mind when I see the Nine of Wands is boundaries. Boundaries are the secret sauce to getting through, finding the stamina to push forward, and defending yourself against those who drain you of energy and time. The Nine of Wands carries the message that you will need to step back and take a break; otherwise, you may risk hurting yourself or derailing your progress. If the work must continue, you may need to call in support or delegate tasks. You may need to establish guidelines as to who has access to your time. Exhaustion is avoidable, but if you push through, you do so at the risk of making errors, and in the end, all that will do is create more work. I notice that the Nine of Wands seems to pop up when I am over-committing or taking on too much. During this time, I tend to become "prickly" in my communications, and although my intention is not to cause harm when feeling overworked and exhausted, sure enough, that is what happens. When the Nine of Wands appears, you may need to step back and ask yourself if you are setting yourself up for either failure or a healthy dose of resentment. Establishing boundaries will help you stay on task as well as keep your relationships intact. Are you trying to be all things to all people, or perhaps are you worried about how some may perceive you if you take time out for yourself? There is no need to play the victim or the Viking because neither one will help you find contentment.The porcupine brings its ability to create an area of protection in the event of any threat approaches. Call on this animal spirit when you need the confidence to stand up for your needs and when you need to feel at ease as it will create a barrier between you and whatever it is that is threatening your success.

Animal Keywords:

Porcupine: Boundaries, safety, protection, humility

TEN OF WANDS

From a distance, an idea you envisioned appeared so easy to reach without obstacles or complications to cause second-thoughts. Now that you are knee-deep and committed, the task is proving to be far more challenging than anticipated. With struggle comes the risk of drowning in self-doubt, of losing passion and enthusiasm for something that once held great promise. The Ten of Wands brings the message that If you want to succeed, you will need to rekindle the fire in your belly to persevere as you are going to encounter a period of struggle before you reach a successful ending. You may also see this as a sign to let go and release yourself from the burden of sticking to a plan as you may come to realize that the struggle or obstacle is far more difficult than the reward should warrant. The Ten of Wands may also point to a situation where you will be the one doing the heavy lifting as others around you wait to benefit from your efforts. Of course, if you fail, it will be on your shoulders to clean up. In Ballard, we have a Salmon ladder that is not only a source of major tourist activity as it is part of the Locks, we locals love it too! Suppose you live in the neighborhood and have small kids. In that case, it is almost obligatory that you bring them to watch the salmon make their way from the Pacific ocean up into Lake Union on their way to their final destination—Lake Washington. I thought about the salmon's long journey when it came time to create the Ten of Wands as this fish carries with it the power of perseverance. Call on the salmon's energy when you need help navigating your way through a difficult or tumultuous situation. Let its spirit help you find the confidence to move forward over each obstacle with a knowing that you have within the power to climb higher, swim longer, and live with purpose.

Animal Keywords:
Salmon: Purpose, determination, renewal, direction,

PAGE OF WANDS

The keywords for the Page of Wands are creative, confident, and enthusiastic. When thinking about these qualities, the bowerbird came right into my mind. This fanciful bird is an artist, it is romantic, it takes animal creativity to a whole new level by creating a work of art that seduces a mate. The bowerbird combs the land looking for bright, glittery complementary objects with an eye towards the aesthetic as it designs an entrance to its nest. When the Page of Wands appears, your current situation will benefit from conjuring up a little enthusiasm, add a little panache. Take a deep breath and call upon that courage you have burning within because it is ready to ignite change. Get excited, get motivated because there is no time to waste—strike now while the iron is hot. If you have been holding back, waiting for some universal green light to let you know it's okay to go ahead with a new idea or opportunity, this is it! You are in a position to make a change. The Page of Wands asks that at this time, you allow your creative mind to explore all options and gravitate towards those that spark passion. When you hold in your heart that you can achieve anything you set out to accomplish, you will find the confidence to take a risk that will lead to success.

If you need inspiration, seek out the energy of the bowerbird as this youthful and this passionate bird will help you find the resources that will not only instill confidence but also attract the opportunity you desire. This bird does not play small; it goes out there with an abundance of chutzpah knowing that it has all that any mate could possibly want, that's the story it tells itself, that's the self-talk that allows it to be vulnerable enough to strut around as if it were a king.

Animal Keywords:

Bowerbird: Creativity, passion, youthfulness, enthusiasm

KNIGHT OF WANDS

The Knight of Wands is adventurous, maybe even a bit overly so at times; he is not a sit on the sidelines kind of fellow waiting for the world to come to him. When the Knight appears, the time for swift, decisive action has arrived, and there is no time for delay. However, the energy this card offers can be conflicting. For success, you will need to strike the perfect balance between persistence and arrogance—between being a go-getter and being a bully.

A situation may have you feeling like you are being pulled in two different directions. There is a charming, passionate side that creates a magnetic enthusiasm that builds support for an idea or purpose. Then there is the arrogant, overly ambitious, restless side that jeopardizes tearing down what the charming and passionate side has built. When the Knight of Wands is present, you can be your own worst enemy! Are you confident in your plans, or are you giving off a cocky or conceited vibe that, in the end, will turn off those whose support you need? The Knight of Wands will give you the sureness to "fake it till you make it" and advises that you create an image in your mind of the person you want to become. Be creative! Be bold! Dig deep and find the courage to play the part because things will fall into place when you do. If your goal is to be a leader at your job, behave the way a leader you would admire would act. It's all about walking the talk.

As I am writing this, reports have come in that for the first time in about 100 years, the wolverine has returned to Mount Rainier. With less than 1,000 wolverines in the lower 48 states, this is pretty exciting. It also means that we still have pockets of land that can support these beautiful creatures.

When you need that little extra kick of tenacity or grit, when you need to be fearless, call upon the wolverine. With its thick, dense, low-center of gravity body, this creature will help you reclaim your balance and connect you to the earth's nurturing energy. With the Wolverine by your side, you will move through your situation with intention, determination, and dominance.

Animal Keywords:
Wolverine: Fearless, aggression, defensive, creative, tenacity

QUEEN OF WANDS

The Queen of Wands saunters in with a sexy, feminine, effervescent energy as she is eager to get out into the world to create something new and magnificent. Her life almost feels boundless! Although often chipper and optimistic, don't mistake her easygoingness with being a push-over or unambitious as this Queen knows what she wants from life, and she knows how to use her charm to secure it. When you encounter the Queen of Wands, you are directed to walk in a leader's shoes, of someone whose mere presence can command the room. This is a woman whose undying upbeat spirit brings a team together with passion and enthusiasm. It is the Queen of Wands who sees the potential in every person and situation and has a knack for drawing out the best in each. When you hold this card in your hand, ask yourself if you are seeing your situation from the Queen of Wands position. Are you able to find the good or the potential just waiting to be discovered? Are you focusing on what is working rather than the flaws? Is your health and well-being a priority?

When you need a boost to your self-esteem when you need to feel powerful and in command, call on the Lioness to help you roar. If you are uncertain or if you feel uneasy about taking the lead, if you need a boost of energy to rally a team, call upon the lioness for her fearlessness and passion. When you walk next to a lioness, you will be protected. The crow is a nod to my first deck, the Crow Tarot. Here this bird is passing the wand to the lioness and with it the power of intuition, of being able to glance through the veil to see all the possibilities the future holds.

Animal Keywords:
Lion: Passion, command, authority, royalty, power, prestige

KING OF WANDS

When I think of the King of Wands, I think of an older, sophisticated, perhaps worldly gentleman who has mastered the balance between being assertive and aggressive. He knows the carrots to dangle in front of a group that will get them energized and excited. He is aware of his voice's power and how to articulate his vision with a sense of drama so that all those within earshot become instantly intrigued. He is debonair, bold, and outspoken, yet at the same time refined and in tune with the room. He knows how to turn on the charisma at just the right time to get what he wants. When you are paid a visit by the King, you are directed to call upon your creativity and channel the entrepreneur within. Your situation will benefit from adding some flair, from taking extra steps that show off your expertise. Your time has come to stand up, stake your claim, and be audacious because when you present your talents to the world, the unique skills you bring to the situation—your originality will be rewarded.

It is not the size of the lion's roar that demands attention and respect; it is the emotion and vision behind it. Use the lion's energy when you need to create a commanding presence when you need a little extra burst of courage to get up in front of a crowd. No one needs to tell the lion he is the King of the Jungle; he knows it deep within, and when you call upon his spirit, you too will be infused with his power, his grace, his passion for living.

Animal Keywords:
Lion: Passion, command, authority, royalty, power, prestige

ACE OF CUPS

The Ace of Cups's message is to see the world from a place of loving divine energy. When you open your heart and experience each moment without prejudice, new opportunities will appear. Get out into nature, appreciate the beauty surrounding you not as a spectator but as a participant—as a contributor to its grace. When you lean into the Ace of Cups's energy, your intuition is heightened, and your higher-self connection is formed. Let go of over-analyzing a situation and let emotion be your guide right now. When you hold the Ace of Cups in your hands, you will feel the loving energy of the Universe. Look for areas where you can connect with someone new who will positively influence your life. This relationship may or may not be romantic, but it will feel secure and karmic.

If you are feeling detached or hurt by someone, look for ways to open the channels for forgiveness as that will help you connect to your inner god/goddess. The black-crowned night heron brings stillness, of moving through nature with grace and ease. These are social birds who spend their days roosting in large communities high up in the trees and their nights alone in North America's wetlands hunting for food. This is a creature at peace with its surroundings and can move between socializing and solitude without friction or discomfort. Lean into the heron's energy when you need patience with yourself and others as this bird will help you go with the flow.

Animal Symbolism:
Heron: Calm, divine energy, balance, quiet

Two of Cups

The elephants stare at each other and with complete precision, and in unison, they fill the other's cup. The Two of Cups brings a bond, which comes from being intuned with another's energy. It is that kind of relationship that just feels right; it is soul-level and karmic. The energy the Two of Cups brings is one that leaves you feeling as though you traveled through lifetimes with someone or held an occupation or passion for something that has moved with you, evolving with each incarnation. This could be a romantic relationship, or it could be a strong friendship or even a deep desire for a particular hobby. It is this person or thing that just fills a void in your soul. When the Two of Cups appears in a reading, you may have a chance encounter with someone who you were destined to know, someone who will feel instantly familiar. You may be on the verge of joining forces with someone who will help your situation improve or grow more sturdy due to their input. If your relationship has been complicated, the two of Cups suggests that you seek out common interests, find ideas or values you share with someone—as your common goals will help you overcome any differences. It seems only fitting for the Two of Cups that the elephant's energy center is in its heart. When you need to feel a sense of belonging, of companionship, call upon this gentle giant to help you connect with your heart center. The elephant brings harmony and emotional intelligence in your situation. Let this magnificent spirit help you find compassion for others and allow its easy nature to soften your spirit. When you connect with the elephant, your heart opens, prejudice and disagreements dissolve, leaving room for new ideas or relationships.

Animal Keywords:
Elephants: Heart-center, relationships, love, harmony, wisdom

THREE OF CUPS

A few years ago, I had a neighbor who would escape the city on the weekends for a cabin out in the woods. One weekend they forgot to lock the doggie door. A family of raccoons seized the very fortuitous opportunity! When it came time to create the Three of Cups, I knew precisely what inspiration I was going to draw upon because, although I did not witness first hand the aftermath, from neighbor accounts, those raccoons worked together to throw quite the party. Can you imagine what it must have felt like for those raccoons? It must have been like winning the lottery.

The Three of Cups speaks to how you feel when you share a time of great joy with others. There is something magical about joining forces with others in celebration, or just working towards a common goal that is sure to be a great success. There is a sense of community and belonging that keeps the passion burning within to keep moving forward. When you encounter the Three of Cups's energy, you will benefit from joining forces with those whose company you enjoy. Chores or tasks will be more fun and more productive when you enlist friends and family to help. Of course, work is always much more pleasurable when it's a work—party! When you hold the Three of Cups, a situation may benefit from asking for help or allowing others interested in your success to become involved. Use your enthusiasm for a project to enlist those who genuinely want to see you succeed. Not only will you gain an eager team ready to get to work—you will find the victory will be sweeter.

If your task requires a hands-on approach, if you need to do physical work, call on the raccoon's energy as this nimble creature possesses a heightened sense of touch. A shapeshifter and natural maker of shenanigans, your situation may benefit from using a little trickery when enlisting friends and family to help with a task, but don't worry, they will thank you in the end for a great time!

Animal Keywords:
Raccoon: Nimble, focused, clever, dexterity

Four of Cups

The Guardian of the Night came to life as a way for me to emotionally manage a new reality of sheltering in place for an undetermined amount of time. There was a great deal of news regarding the pangolin and perhaps its ties to the Coronavirus during March. Admittedly, I didn't know much about this truly unique and reclusive creature other than it was prized for its meat in some areas of the world. The pangolin, as a method of hiding from poachers, rolls itself into a ball. Sadly though, by doing this, the pangolin is more manageable to catch and transport. For a creature so coveted, there isn't much information out there other than it is known for its hard scaly exterior. An exterior that those of considerable means once used to create battle-ready armor. Despite the limited information, when it came time to make the Four of Cups, I knew exactly who would fit this energy. When the Four of Cups appears, you may be allowing emotions to drive you into a defensive position. Afraid of exposing your feelings or being vulnerable, you may feel inclined to curl up in a ball, go within, and isolate yourself from others. During this time, your sole focus is only your needs, your desire to avoid discomfort, your fear of being exposed, and much like the pangolin, your first instinct may be to hide.

You may tell yourself that the world around you can wait until these emotions subside. If you use this time to your advantage, you may discover a new perspective or see your situation from a different angle; however, if you use this time purely to escape reality, you will find only stagnation. Or worse, someone may catch on to the fact you are avoiding something. You may also want to consider if you are letting your emotions cloud your vision, are you missing a significant opportunity? The pangolin offers it's large, protective, keratin scales to help you create space to be alone, a place for you to go within and consider your next move.

Animal Keywords:
Pangolin: Protection, going inward, curling up, introverted

FIVE OF CUPS

The Five of Cups may point to an upcoming disappointment or loss as it bears the message that feelings associated with misfortune loom in the darkness. This card may also point to a previous setback or a loss currently consuming space in your heart. As a result, you are not capable of moving on or making room for all that you have in life to appreciate. It is here that you may find yourself stuck in a state of grief. Allow yourself time to process your emotions. Feel anger, feel despair, let sadness have its moment. The Five of Cups asks that you accept the loss and acknowledge the pain and suffering you feel within but for balance to be restored, you must let go of what can not be repaired. Holding on to the past will not help you move forward; it will only create more suffering.

The site of a Death's-head hawk moth is imposing and can be alarming! A symbol of bad things to come, this migratory moth once tormented the mentally fragile King George III when two appeared in his bedroom. Those who have seen Silence of the Lambs will recognize this moth from the movie. Although not sinister in the slightest, this moth has gained a reputation for being a bad omen. Like all moths, the Death's-head hawk moth is drawn to light; use this instinct to help you find the good in others or a source of inspiration that will lighten your day. A less flashy relative of the butterfly, moths, can blend in and camouflage themselves. Call on this energy if you need to deal with people who may be less sympathetic to your situation as it will help you avoid any feelings of being attacked.

Animal Keywords:
Death's head hawk moth: Mystery, loss, transformation, camouflage

Six of Cups

Remember the days when you would wake up, and your only responsibility was to play. For many of us, that may seem like a lifetime ago! Life was easy, it was carefree—it was fun. Each day held new and exciting possibilities for amusement. When it was time to go to sleep, it was the simple joys of life that left you feeling cared for and content. That is the energy of the Six of Cups; it is the sentiment of childhood innocence. When I read for myself and this card appears, I know I have been taking life a little too seriously, and it is time to get outside with my daughter for some goofing off. Aside from the quality time, an hour or so of play can lead to several hours of productive work that I wouldn't have had without a break.

It's hard not to be in a blissful state when you are outside playing, and it is that state of being that you open the channel for positive encounters and new ideas. When you draw the Six of Cups, your situation may benefit from taking your inner-child out on a playdate. Depending on your situation, however, you may also need to consider if you are not taking responsibility or playing the innocent as a means to avoid any feelings of guilt.

The high-spirited young elephants are in the happiness-zone with their trunks "in the air like they just don't care," focusing their energy on the simple pleasures that come from being in the water. Elephants have this larger than life natural, cheerful quality, and vibrantly express happiness when they play. When you feel uneasy about letting loose or feel the burdens and responsibilities of adult life zapping your positive energy, call upon the elephant. This wise animal will help you strike the perfect balance between work and play. A powerful force in body and in mind, the elephant, will help you break through obstacles that may be preventing you from enjoying the simple pleasures of life.

Animal Keywords:
Elephants: Heart-center, relationships, love, harmony, wisdom

SEVEN OF CUPS

There is a fine line between dreaming big and becoming lost in a fantasy. The Seven of Cups asks that you allow your mind room to wander amongst the stars without restriction; however, you must remain aware of where your feet are planted. When we dream big, our creative mind expands, allowing for more opportunities. However, the difference between dreaming and living in a fantasy world is action. When you take steps to bring a dream to life, it transforms into a goal, something far more powerful, and —you increase your odds of making it real.The Seven of Cups may indicate a situation that may be limited due to your inability to envision something more extraordinary. You may feel as though it is not possible, and as a result, a restriction is created. When you allow yourself to feel worthy of grand events or desires, your opportunities will become only limited by your imagination. However, the Seven of Cups may indicate you are spending too much time daydreaming about what could be instead of focusing on the present moment. Without action, you are no closer to achieving your goal by merely envisioning it.

When it comes time to increase your potential, to manifest abundance, the rabbit's energy is ready to help you create! The rabbit brings fertility to your situation and the ability to produce new opportunities. In stories, it is the rabbit that often serves as a guide, leading to great adventures! Call on the rabbit when you feel lost in a field of possibilities or unsure of which path to take as it will show you the direction that will yield the greatest results.

Animal Keywords:
Rabbit: Abundance, reproduction, open, creativity, luck

EIGHT OF CUPS

The inspiration for the Eight of Cups came from the BBC series Planet Earth II the cities episode. This fascinating episode captured falcons thriving in New York, leopards running Mumbai's streets, and so many more animals who have adapted and found space in sprawling cities.

The Eight of Cups brings to the surface feelings that arise from examining your current status in life and discovering something is missing. There is almost a hollowness that comes with the energy of the Eight of Cups. An emptiness that is waiting to be filled. You may notice that your current situation no longer leaves you feeling nourished or excited. This card is not all doom and gloom; quite on the contrary, what it does is offers a glimpse of a brighter future of greater possibilities that are waiting in the distance. When you draw this card, you may already know that there is a grander opportunity out there, but you may need to abandon something challenging to release in moving forward. The way I approach the Eight of Cups's energy is that it is the energy that comes from graduating or moving away from a situation you have outgrown. There is a part of you that doesn't want to change because your current situation is so familiar, so comfortable, it's easy, but in the end, you know that the time has come to say goodbye and embark on a new path. You may love a job that you have held for years without a promotion. You may have created bonds with your co-workers, but when the possibilities are slim for any advancement and the feeling that surfaces thanks to the Eight of Cups is one that leaves you teetering between anticipation and dread, you will know a change is needed.

The mighty jaws of the tiger can crush just about anything, yet at the same time, the tiger's mouth is gentle enough to carry its young. Use the power of the tiger to claim your future while maintaining control of your emotions. When you call upon the tiger, you will be amiable, yet firm in your decision-making. Tigers have a regal, graceful quality; they are true leaders and possess a strength that commands respect. Use this energy when you need to communicate your plans for the future with others, and you will notice that the support you have enjoyed will move with you when you move forward.

Animal Keywords:
Tiger: Strength, nobility, emotions

NINE OF CUPS

The wish card. The Nine of Cups is a license to kick back and enjoy life! Look at what you have been able to achieve. Can you feel a sense of pride? Take a moment to spread your feathers and show the world the awesomeness that is you! Don't be shy; you have worked hard and are now in a position of feeling complete and total satisfaction. Take a moment to exhale and appreciate the rewards that have come from all the hard work you invested! There will be time to get back to business but for now, enjoy some of the abundances you created. The Nine of Cups asks that you lean deep into the feeling that comes from receiving a desire or having a wish fulfilled.

The peacock can change its appearance dramatically just by opening up its feathers, and as a result, our perception of the bird changes as well. It instantly becomes more prominent, more vibrant, and more impressive to watch. The peacock's energy will help you show off your flashy side, that part of you that exudes passion and is self-assured.

When a situation requires a boost of confidence and feelings of pride, call on the peacock. This energy comes in especially handy during a job interview when you need to boast or articulate your success to others or when when you meet your ex's new partner. When you need to show that you deserve to have the attention of all the room's eyes, this energy will put your brilliance on display, and others will take notice.

Animal Keywords:
Peacock: Showy, pride, passion, sensuality

TEN OF CUPS

The Ten of Cups carries feelings of happiness and contentment with life. It is an energy created from the simple joys from being in harmony with those within your community and nature. The Ten of Cups can indicate that a problematic situation is ending, opening the door for a peaceful time in your life. Moments of stress or struggle will be replaced by feelings of optimism and bliss. When you lean into the Ten of Cups's energy, you will find it easy to connect emotionally with those around you who you cherish. Suppose you are experiencing conflict or a difficult situation—lean into the Ten of Cups's energy. You will naturally create a bridge between differences so that common ground can be found. Finding the emotional strength to extend an olive branch will have lasting positive effects. Focus your energy on what you have in common rather than where your differences keep you apart. The Ten of Cups's message is that we all gain when we work together to create an atmosphere that promotes peace and harmony.The forest animals come together for the Ten of Cups as they are a community that brings their unique talents and resources to support each other.

Page of Cups

If there is one word that ties together the energy of the Page of Cups and the capybara, it is loving. The power you hold in your hands when you draw the Page of Cups card is one that will help you find the good in others; it will help you mend broken relationships and form romantic bonds. If you are dealing with a difficult situation or someone who is let's say "challenging" to be polite when the Page of Cups appears, you are best served by taking a softer, more gentle approach. Tap into your intuition, get a feel for the energy you are dealing with, and work to ease friction instead of irritating it. When you encounter the Page of Cups, expect inspiration to come from unexpected places as it relaxes our biases, and opens our hearts. That person you discounted yesterday may turn around to be a valuable source of information that will help overcome an obstacle. Before I began the illustration for the Page of Cups, I researched "friendly" animals, and the capybara topped the list as the friendliest creature on the planet! They are also the largest rodent in the world and can weigh up to 150lbs! These semi-aquatic social creatures possess a calmness that comes from being comfortable wherever they go; the world is their playground. Other animals in the area, perhaps, taking advantage of the good-natured capybara, will hop on its back for a free ride across rivers and streams. Because the capybara lives along the shoreline, dividing their time between the river and land they pull together the elements of water and earth to create an animal that is emotionally sensitive to others' needs while at the same time grounded and confident in its position. If you feel out of balance, or disconnected from your soul center, call on the capybara as this loving energy will be your guide and help you find your way across flooded emotions.

Animal Keywords: Capybara: Friendly, compassionate, kind

KNIGHT OF CUPS

The Knight of Cups is a charmer, and the person or situation who holds this energy has the power to create the perfect distraction when an emotional lift is needed. Magic seems to happen when you open your heart to the Knight of Cups, as the feeling of butterflies in your stomach and anticipation create a frequency that attracts romance and new connections. Love in the air! Like all Knights, the Knight of Cups is a complicated fellow. One minute he is passionately talking about something of interest, and the next minute he's alone brooding. This Knight's goal is to strike a balance, of being free with your heart, and open to new experiences without being irrational or temperamental. You may find yourself becoming a bit more emotional or sensitive, and as a result, you will need to ask yourself how this energy is impacting your situation. Are you passionate or obsessive? Are you taking things seriously or being overly sensitive? When the Knight of Cups appears in a reading, you may want to consider if your situation may benefit from seeking out someone with a creative flair, someone with the ability to charm a room. One thing to keep in mind is that the Knight of Cups may be the lift you need at the moment; this energy is not stable, nor is it one that serves a successful foundation too often. If you are assisted by someone with the energy of the Knight of Cups, be grateful for their contribution but know that you will need to finish the job in the end. Love begins within. The beautiful and almost angelic swan brings to the Knight of Cups grace and serenity. When called upon, it will help you temper any volatile situations that may result from emotions running a muck. Use the swan's light energy when you need to neutralize a heated situation to restore peace or when you need to connect with someone who is emotionally closed off. Animal Keywords: Swan: Love, grace, bonding

QUEEN OF CUPS

When the Queen of Cups is present, she creates an energy within a situation that promotes unity and agreement. She instantly connects with the vibration that fills a room and feels the emotions of others deeply. Their happiness is her happiness, their pain is her pain. Her insight into others' feelings creates empathy and allows her to open her heart to those who need her most. Like a caring mother, she applies comfort and understanding. She knows when to talk and when it is best to simply be a shoulder to cry on.

When the Queen of Cups is present, your situation will improve or benefit from expressing love and tuning into the emotions of those around you. It is time to step into this gentle Queen's shoes and put aside personal desires and focus on how those around you feel; doing so will create harmony and promote a positive shift.

The Queen of Cups is an energy that sends its power outward instead of drawing it in, the Queen focuses her efforts on healing others first, knowing she has more than enough emotional strength to share. Dive deep and feel the rhythm of the water around you. Can you feel its vibration? The orca's energy focuses on creating peace within a family and being intuned with those closest to you. When you connect with the orca, you will find the strength to console others while remaining unsinkable. Giving your time and energy to others will not drain your life-force as the orca is present to ensure that the healing you give flows in a circle, going out as it is restored within.

Animal Keywords:
Orca: Deep emotions, family, connection, intuition

KING OF CUPS

The King of Cups knows that when the water is choppy, when the sand from the bottom is stirred up, it is harder to find the fish, it is harder to eat. When the water is calm, that is when he will feast. The King of Cups's energy is tolerant of differences and offers a warm, compassionate reception to all he encounters. It is his energy that establishes a soothing atmosphere as he focuses his attention on fostering harmonious relationships. When the king is present, you will benefit from favoring diplomacy and compromise over conflict and aggression.

The King of Cups asks that you step up and take on a mediator's role, of a leader who genuinely cares for those who seek wisdom. If you find yourself in a situation where everyone is at loggerheads and communication has broken down, the King of Cups will help you find the insight and compassion to ease conflict. When you use your intuition and emotional intelligence to find solutions that reduce disagreement and quiet discourse, you will be recognized as a leader who cares about ensuring all parties benefit.

Call on the orca when you need to rise above the drama. When you need to go into a situation that requires a deep understanding of all involved positions and still be able to breathe, the orca will assist you. This noble and playful king of the ocean knows how to cut through even the choppiest of emotional waves and provide you with the insight that will direct your energy towards finding a peaceful outcome.

Animal Keywords:
Orca: Deep emotions, family, connection, intuition

ACE OF SWORDS

Life is going to throw you a curveball. When the Ace of Swords's energy is present, you will have the clarity to see an obstacle forming, you will know that you will need to plan for a challenge. The Ace of Swords calls on you to seek out the truth behind your circumstances. Use your logical mind to find the answers. When you see your situation objectively, you will better understand your role, and as a result, you will be able to move with swift determination to resolve any conflict. This is a challenge that with preparation and commitment, you will win. When the Ace of Swords appears, your situation will benefit from a little honesty. It may not be easy, but you will find those who can support your cause will listen when you speak your truth. Lean into the Ace of Swords's energy when you need to clearly articulate your needs, express with certainty, and operate from a place of integrity. The Ace of Swords brings one warning, be careful of illusions that may mask themselves as answers as they may cloud your vision. You will benefit from using a combination of logic and intuition.The bat's superpower is the ability to travel across the darkest of skies with precision and grace. Call on the bat's energy when you need to navigate through any moments of darkness when you need to hone in on a clear path to success. When you connect with the bat, you tune in to your intuition, you can feel the vibration around you, and making quick, decisive decisions will come naturally. The bat offers grace and flexibility and will guide you when you need to change course on short notice or if you are expected to fly higher than anticipated.The grasshopper is a symbol of being true to yourself, of living your life, not imitating others as your life is about to take a leap forward.

Animal Keywords:
Bat: Magical, intuitive, quiet, esoteric, success, prosperity

Two of Swords

The poor frog is stuck on two swords sticking up out of the water. Of course, if you ask this frog, it will tell you everything is fine; it's just hanging out. But in reality, it can't see land, and the fog that hovers above the water reveals only murky shadows of what may be potential threats, and this frog is scared to death. The energy of the Two of Swords is one that carries indecision, of avoiding discomfort because you do not have enough information to make a choice. Fear of being injured or making the wrong move is creating a barrier blocking you from moving forward. The Two of Swords may indicate that you know exactly what needs to be done; however, emotionally, you are not ready to acknowledge the truth. As a result, you find yourself mentally unable to deal with responsibility.

You may be consciously choosing to stay in the dark if others around you possess the information that would require you to take action that results in losing a comfortable position. Ignorance can be bliss, but rarely does it help a situation advance. The frog represents prosperity and new life. A master at transformation, this creature has moved up and out of the mud and into the clear night sky.

Call on the frog when events require you to take a frightening leap or take you out of your comfort zone. When you connect with this energy, not only will you enjoy the benefits of change, you will spark a transformation within that will open the doors for new and fortuitous possibilities.

Animal Keywords:
Frog: Growth, balance, prosperity, transformation, good-fortune

THREE OF SWORDS

When I created the Three of Swords, I wanted you to feel a heaviness that none of the other cards possess. When you hold this card, can you feel the low rumbling vibration? This is an energy that comes from feeling betrayed, of knowing that your trust has been violated, of being so painfully aware that you are not the victor but rather the victim. It is the energy that comes from discovering your husband or wife cheated on you for years, or that your business partner cooked the books and left you holding the bag. It is the energy that comes from learning you lost a promotion because of a backstabbing co-worker. I have found that this card seems to make its way into readings when there is a breach of trust within a partnership or group. It may not indicate an ending, but it does represent a growing problem that needs to be resolved to mend the relationship.

When The Three of Swords appears, you may need to be painfully honest with yourself and acknowledge an area in your life that you know is not right, that something is amiss. Those of you who know me will tell you, I always look for something positive even in the Three of Swords, and if there is one good thing that can be said about this card, it is that from the moment you cross this energy, the process of healing can begin. There is absolute freedom that comes from knowing where you stand in a situation, of no longer being in the dark or played for a fool. When I thought about the heaviness of the Three of Swords's energy and how it would relate in a deck full of beautiful creatures, my mind went straight to the poaching of elephant tusks, something that continues today. I thought about the bond between humans and elephants and how greedy and cruel a person must be to break that trust.

The elephant energy is grounded and focused on establishing an unshakable family bond; it is there strength resides. When your heart is aching, when you feel betrayed, call on the elephant to help you connect with your family, to help you find loving support that will protect and heal your broken heart. Intelligent and courageous, the elephant will guide you towards rational and logical solutions when it is time to move forward.

Animal Keywords:
Elephants: Heart-center, relationships, love, harmony, wisdom

FOUR OF SWORDS

After creating the emotionally draining Three of Swords, I needed to find a creature that would be a bit more uplifting and fun for the Four of Swords, and the cute little hedgehog fit the bill.

When the Four of Swords appears, you may find it beneficial to take a step back and seek out space away from distractions for a little quiet contemplation. You may be experiencing a bombardment of input coming in from those around you who are pushing an agenda or offering unsolicited guidance or advice. However, as helpful those around you may consider themselves to be, at this time, you will find the solution you need resides within. Seek a peaceful place away from any chatter and listen to your inner voice. It will be your intuition, the wisdom you hold within that will provide you with the best guidance. The Four of Swords asks that you prioritize self-care, rest your mind and your body. By establishing boundaries and demanding some personal space, you will free yourself from others' emotional demands, allowing you to focus your valuable energy on conceiving and executing a plan for growth and success.

Hedgehogs know the value of getting some much-needed rest and in the wild, they hibernate during the winter months. This soft, fuzzy creature will be there when you need some pampering when you need to wrap yourself up and escape the modern world. The hedgehog's divine feminine energy creates a space of warmth and protection as it supports your need for rest. When you work with the hedgehog, it will help you defend yourself against any time bandits or emotional vampires. Call on the hedgehog when you need to establish respected but not off-putting or destructive boundaries to relationships.

Animal Keywords:
Hedgehog: Survival, going inward, boundaries, rest

FIVE OF SWORDS

The Five of Swords indicates you are in one of three positions. The first is that of a brute, the person who sees something they want and simply takes it without considering the impact of their actions. You may have made gains through less than honorable tactics, but be warned any victory will be hollow and your reputation damaged. The second position is that of the enabler or someone complicit. Perhaps you benefited in some way by the dishonorable actions of another. You may not have done the dirty work, but you did reap some reward as a result. Although you were not directly involved, your inaction will leave you weakened as others will recognize your lack of integrity.

The final position is that of the victim or the sufferer as a result of the actions of the selfish. Your well-being, opinions, or requirements were never even on the table; they were never even considered. And yet, you are the one who is negatively affected.

The Five of Swords asks you to acknowledge your role in the situation, what is your contribution because once you establish your role, you will know what action to take.

The story of the deer on the Five of Swords is one that is not uncommon. The land is bulldozed, trees are toppled, and buildings are erected. All of this is done without too often considering the animals impacted by business leaders and developers' decisions; they are the decision-makers. Or worse, considered and utterly disregarded. If you find yourself surrounded by the Five of Swords's energy, call on the deer for support as this animal will help you find the confidence to confront your situation head-on. To survive, deer use their ability to feel vibration and follow their instinct. When you use the deer's power, you will have a sense of what is right and what is wrong, your intuition will guide you towards inner peace.

Animal Keywords:
Deer: Intuition, confidence, protection

SIX OF SWORDS

The Six of Swords carries an energy that is slightly dispirited. It's the energy present on cold grey Sunday afternoons during the winter months when I wonder why I moved to Seattle and not someplace sunnier. There really isn't anything bad happening, but there also isn't much excitement—either way, life is moving on, and it isn't horrible. A situation that didn't pan out how you had hoped may trigger moments of regret, but with acceptance, the past will drift away, and a new adventure will begin to unfurl. The Six of Swords asks that you give space and time for low-vibrational feelings time to surface so that you can gain a clear vision for a more positive path.

You may not be experiencing a great deal of enthusiasm, but at least you are moving in the right direction.

When you need to feel at peace at a slower pace, when you need to feel protected from negative self-talk or outside influences that jeopardize perseverance, call upon the turtle. A creature that can ride the waves and follow the currents for thousands of miles knows a thing or two about patience and letting go of a need for speed. The turtle asks that you use this time to gain perspective and not rush through life; otherwise, you may miss some crucial moments.

Animal Keywords:
Turtle: Persistence, direction, protection, patience

SEVEN OF SWORDS

The Seven of Swords suggests a situation may test your honor and integrity. If you are tempted to abandon the insights and wisdom of those around you, the result may be the perception that you are arrogant and self-serving. Be aware of your self-talk when you draw the Seven of Swords. Are you convinced that you are the only one with the skills or the knowledge to handle a situation or bring about success? Although your efforts may not be motivated by selfishness, in the end you also may not receive many thank-yous as you expected. The energy the Seven of Swords brings is that of solitude and independence—of going it alone.

Not always negative; this energy, when used appropriately, can be beneficial if you are working with a group of people who are disinterested and ineffectual as you will have the confidence to move forward without worrying about the feelings of others who are slacking.

Be aware that The Seven of Swords supports an atmosphere where accountability is easily hidden. If you or someone else manages all the details alone without oversight, there is a possibility of deception or cutting corners without acknowledgment. Found in the Americas, the black panther, like other jaguars, lives a solitary life on the top of the food chain. The only threat to these beautiful and powerful creatures are humans. Call on the panther's energy when you need to fill the role of a leader that commands respect as it will help you maintain your integrity and honesty. If you need to confront a difficult situation that leaves you frightened of the consequences, the fearless panther will be your guide over this obstacle as it will show you the path towards honor and dignity. When you confront your fears, traveling into the darkness within, uncovering that part of yourself that is all too comfortable with staying hidden, you will unleash an awakening, and your life will change for the better.

Animal Keywords:
Panther: Independence, pride, strength, intuition, survival

EIGHT OF SWORDS

For the Eight of Swords, I wanted to take a different approach from how the traditional Rider-Waite-Smith decks (including my past decks) illustrate this energy and focus on the feeling of powerlessness and confusion from the first-person perspective. The person who holds the card is trapped in a hole, looking upward and immobilized. Although it was not the first card I created for this deck, it is the first one that came into my mind over a year ago. I loved the idea of putting the reader in the deck.

When the Eight of Swords appears, it brings to our attention an area in our lives where we feel powerless or trapped.

The situation may be a relationship that you stay in for no other reason other than it is too expensive to go out on your own. It is a time of feeling in limbo, unable to move and, at the same time, unable to figure out what to do next as options are not readily available. The Eight of Swords suggest that perhaps you dug yourself into a hole, and now you need to find some clarity to get out. You may notice the options you once held are no longer available. For example, if you stayed in a job because it paid the bills expecting to move into your dream job later on down the road, that option may be quickly waning as you are no longer perceived as a viable candidate for the position. Circling above, you are three owls, and although they may appear menacing, they are there to help you uncover your inner-wisdom, feel protected, and gain a different perspective. Within us are all the answers to the mysteries of the world. Call on the owl to help you feel confident in your wisdom. You hold the power to move forward and find solutions that ease restriction and create happiness. The owl will help you build trust in the knowledge you have within to see the abundance of opportunities where you once saw none.

Animal Keyword:
Owl: Wisdom, protection, authority, awareness, guidance

NINE OF SWORDS

As a parent, I have encountered the energy of the Nine of Swords first hand. The Nine of Swords's energy can seem to linger in the air, just waiting for the right moment to strike. It is a force that stokes fear and anxiety; it is the energy that prompts new parents to hold a mirror under their newborn's nose to make sure it is breathing in the middle of the night. When I created the Nine of Swords, I thought about how we second guess ourselves and our actions not because we worry about our own needs but rather those we love. Did we do everything right? Could things have gone better if a different decision was made? I envisioned a polar bear mother looking out into a melting landscape with brown skies created by pollution, wondering if there is a better place to move with her child, or is this as good as it gets? This brings a combination of guilt and worry that can be paralyzing. When the Nine of Swords appears, you may want to consider if you are worrying to the point of creating undue anxiety. Are you overthinking a situation and causing yourself unnecessary stress? Although this is not my favorite card to come up when doing a reading, it does serve a valuable purpose as it illuminates areas where we seem to get in our own way, where we fret so much over something to the point that we can actually attract the problem we would like to avoid. The energy of the bear is one that will help you find a good night's sleep as it creates comfort within your mind and protects you from negative or anxious thoughts. The polar bear's fur is not white but rather transparent, reflecting the light. Its black skin absorbs the energy of the sun. Call on the polar bear when you need inner-compassion and patience as it will help you feel connected with the loving touch of mother earth.

Animal Keyword:

Bear: Rest, renewal, guidance, inner-peace

TEN OF SWORDS

During the early months of the pandemic, my daughter and I watched our fair share of movies. One movie, in particular, had a significant impact on how I approached the Ten of Swords was Vivarium. I can't say Vivarium was worthy of an Oscar, but it was interesting and did teach me about parasitic brooders. The Ten of Swords's energy brings an atmosphere that creates a feeling within that comes from being on the receiving end of an attack. You may feel as though someone is trying to push you out or take over your rightful position, and as a result, you find yourself in a state of victimhood. The Ten of Swords may indicate an event in the near future that will result in suffering at the hands of someone who uses your weakness to their advantage to further their position. Although this card is not one that many like to see, it can be one that opens our eyes and allows us to reflect upon our role in the situation. Are we really the one who is being brushed aside or are we playing the martyr's role? Do you find yourself giving in to others' desires only to turn around and complain about how your needs are always second? If there is one thing to be said about the Ten of Swords is once you hit bottom, once the deed is done, it is over and resides in the past. Any replaying of the anguish will be not at the hand of the perpetrator but rather your own. The yellow warbler is often the victim of the imposing cowbird who sees an opportunity of passing off the job of parenthood. Over time, the warbler has learned to create a barrier of grass between the cowbird eggs and its own eggs to ensure that the cowbird does not hatch. The lesson we can learn from the warbler is how to deal with those who wish to take advantage of our good nature. This bird has mastered the art of creating boundaries!

Animal Keyword:

Warbler: Progress, nurturing, ideas, expansion

Page of Swords

For the Page of Swords, I chose the Black-Footed Ferret, thanks to a backer's suggestion. This adorable creature is also one of the most endangered and was once considered to be extinct! Well. The Page of Swords is about fortitude, and well, I think climbing your way back from extinction shows a whole lot of fortitude!

The Page of Swords has the heart of an activist as passion, conviction, and a quest for truth collide. When this card appears, it may signal a situation requiring you to confront a difficulty or get out of your comfort zone. The Page energy creates tests or lessons that stimulate growth. When combined with a sword's energy, your test centers around beliefs, your ability to see a situation clearly, and/or your ability to speak truth to power. This hurdle may seem overwhelming at times; however, if you possess the mental grit to find success, the wisdom you gain from this experience will create a whole new world of opportunities. The Page of Swords represents youthful energy and may also indicate that although you are passionate about fighting for something you believe in, there is a risk of being perceived as immature or possessing a childlike idealism.

The ferret brings a playful quality and is known for its inquisitive nature. Call upon the ferret when you need to win over others as this curious creature will provide you with the energy to do your research. When you call upon the ferret, you find engagement with others will yield important information as you will find the questions to the answers that will solve your problems will pop right into your head.

Animal Keyword:
Ferret: Curiosity, playfulness, resourceful

KNIGHT OF SWORDS

Okay, take a moment, get the song out of your head....aaahhh barracuda!

Have you ever encountered a person who is as sharp as a tack, someone who can grasp the most complex of subjects within a few minutes and, at the same time, seems to lack any sense of humility or compassion? This is a person who may not be aware of how opinionated they come off or how sharp their words cut. When someone is focused on the facts and only the facts, social cues go out the door. Tact is not their forte, to say the least. When you need to comprehend a situation or understand a contract, the Swords's energy will help you cut through any brain fog. This energy will also make it much easier to be decisive and confident in your decision, knowing it is, after all, the most logical choice. Too much time with the Knight of Swords, however, will leave others feeling a bit chaffed as your social skills will be seen as lacking. If you need to go into a legal proceeding and have let emotions dictate your strategy so far when the Knight of Swords appears, it will be time to put feelings aside and focus only on the facts.

The barracuda is ruthless, stealthy, and fast. They cut through the water with precision and clarity as they go after their prey. Call on the barracuda when you require feeling powerful and sharp. The barracuda is also a master of patience and will help you ease your mind while you are waiting for the perfect moment to strike.

Animal Keyword:
Barracuda: Sharp, patient, focused, disguises itself

QUEEN OF SWORDS

The Queen of Swords rises high, creating a barrier between herself and all the noise that may cloud her judgment. From this place of clarity, she understands her role and the role others play in an outcome. Her wit is one of her greatest assets. She has an uncanny ability to lighten the mood with humor without diminishing the circumstances' seriousness if the situation becomes tense or, worse, awkward. When stepping into the Queen of Swords's shoes, you will discover an ability to quickly size up a situation as her influence will help you cut through any superfluous information that may be creating indecision. When you encounter the Queen of Swords, you are asked to examine your situation from a place of honesty—not what you hope will happen, but rather what is happening in real-time. Are you truthful with yourself and others? Stand tall and self-assured, just as the Queen would stand, have the courage to speak up knowing that others will respect your integrity. When you take on the Queen of Swords's role, you will see the world free from illusion, and those around you who may try to trick or deceive you will be quickly spotted and called out. Lean on this energy when you need to engage with others who may be less than honest as you will swiftly size up their game so that you are the winner.

The energy center for the owl is the crown. Hold your head high and know that you are being guided by an intelligent and intuitive power animal. Call on the owl's wisdom to help you see your situation from a different angle and from a distance that offers you a clear look at the entire landscape, not just a small portion.

Animal Keyword:
Owl: Wisdom, protection, authority, awareness, guidance

KING OF SWORDS

The King of Swords possesses everything one would expect from a leader. He is analytical and just, giving all parties space to make their case. When speaking, the King is articulate and consciously communicates to a broad audience ensuring his message is understood. He is passionate about maintaining fairness and equality, leaving his personal opinions out of the decision making process.

When the King of Swords appears in a reading, you may find your situation will benefit from taking the King's actions by making time to research all the facts before a final decision is made. If you are working within a team, allow others space to make their case before casting down a ruling or making your opinions known. Are you letting your emotions impact your decision or are you staying impartial? Do you encourage others to rise up to a higher standard by demonstrating your own high integrity level?

Like the Queen of Swords, the owl king also provides you with a powerful animal guide. Call on the owl when you need to clear the air and when you need to be impartial. The owl is here to protect you from caving into your emotions or those of others that may lead to favoring a side out of fear of retribution and not facts.

Animal Keyword:
Owl: Wisdom, protection, authority, awareness, guidance

ACE OF PENTACLES

You are planting the seeds today for long-term goals that will blossom over time. Listen to your intuition as it will be a guiding force and will move you in the right direction. The Ace of Pentacles serves as a reminder that small, purposeful actions taken today will blossom into something fruitful in the future. Have patience; it takes time for seeds to sprout. You are in the beginning phases of a transformation process, and it will be a process and not some overnight windfall, but stay focused on the goal, and it will bear fruit.

When the Ace of Pentacles appears, I get all a flutter inside because I know that the possibilities are out there, that there is potential to bring something marvelous into this world, all I have to do is put in the work. It's an incredible feeling knowing that you have the power to create something, to bring something you desire into fruition. Use that energy you get when you hold this card to come up with practical steps to lead you down the path to creating success.

The powerful and intuitive owl will help you see the opportunities that may have gone unnoticed or underappreciated. Use this energy to create light within a situation that will lead to seeing the whole picture and seeing not only what is present now but also what will be available to you in the future.

Animal Keyword:
Owl: Wisdom, protection, authority, awareness, guidance

Two of Pentacles

You tackled your first handful of tasks by 10am, you are moving through the day with relative ease despite the full plate and what seems to be a growing to-do list; yet, you somehow found a way to remain cheerful, that is the energy of the Two of Pentacles. Oh, I can tell you there are days when leaning into the Two of Pentacles's energy saves me from dropping, not just a ball or two, but the whole dang circus!

When you encounter this card in a reading, your situation may call for a bit more flexibility and a healthy dose of inner-compassion as you keep life in balance.

The dolphin is a natural protector and known for rescuing sailors who have fallen into the water (perhaps also a metaphor for those who fall too deep into their emotions?). Call upon this nurturing protector of the sea to help you regain your strength. These loving and curious animals bring a blend of compassion and logic to your situation and will help you discover a way to smoothly cruise through any difficult day.

Animal Keyword:
Dolphin: Play, swimming through life, enthusiasm

Three of Pentacles

A wolf is going to be a wolf, and like all of us, it needs sustenance to survive—of the last check, I haven't encountered any stories of vegan wolves. The wolves come to the Three of Pentacles to tell a story of teamwork and being in sync with others when pursuing a common goal. Each member of the pack has a role to play and each one is just as important as the next. A leader brings planning, but it is only with the support of the others that the group eats.

The Three of Pentacles asks that you consider your options and what resources you have available to aid in your success. This is not a time to run in without any ideas and hope for the best; no, this is time to calculate each move, pull together a team of skilled partners, and focus your energy on executing a flawless plan. Call on the guidance of the wolf when you need to trust those in your pack. Delegating tasks can be difficult, and letting go of control can be downright scary, but you feel protected with the wolf leading the way.

Use the wolf to help you connect with your intuition so that you can trust your instincts. When you walk alongside the wolf's spirit, you walk in balance, with confidence and no longer in survival mode but with a grace and ease that comes from inner-strength.

Animal Keyword:
Wolf: Family, reliance, hope, teamwork, confidence
Deer: Intuition, confidence, protection

Four of Pentacles

When it came time to create an image for the Four of Pentacles, I thought about the nimble fox losing its agility because it is consumed by the fear of failing to keep the quick-moving rabbits it caught earlier in the evening. In trying to restrict the rabbits, it also restricts itself.

When the Four of Pentacles appears, you may need to examine how control or your need for it impacts a situation. Are you or someone else holding on to something so tightly that there is no room for growth? An example of this may be someone who cannot let go of some tasks at work, who is unwilling to relinquish control to a co-worker or hire help. This may, in the end, cause stagnation or less productivity. The question you may want to ask yourself is are you saving or investing. One grows, the other stays the same.

The rabbit brings abundance, call on this energy but don't restrict it, let it run free. Release the fox to do what it does best, be nimble and clever. When you use the fox and the rabbit in harmony, you will have the skills needed to bring about a positive shift and, with it, a bountiful harvest.

Animal Keyword:
Rabbit: Abundance, reproduction, open, creativity, luck
Fox: Cleverness, spry, magical, shape shifting

FIVE OF PENTACLES

In a world where support should be abundant, where the powerful should help others rise up but instead block the way, the Five of Pentacles indicates a time when you may feel more like the prey instead of the predator. The caterpillar wants nothing more than fulfilling its destiny and moving into a state of metamorphosis; however, blocking the path is an owl, the symbol of wisdom, a symbol of authority and power. You may be experiencing a time of difficulty when you lack the resources you need to thrive. This energy leads to a downward spiral quickly if left unchecked, one that will have you feeling like an outcast or not accepted. It starts with a loss of a job or income, then it's the inability to care for your health; before long, the troubles mount, and finding a path back is more challenging but not impossible as with everything in life, this too shall pass. Usually, this card comes as a warning, as a signal that you are straying into an area that may lead to a series of unfortunate events. Be aware of how setbacks are influencing your life. Are you patient with yourself? Do you see the opportunity to grow from the experience? Are you able to see beyond your current troubles?

Call on the caterpillar when you need trust in the process, when you need the patience to give events that will turn your life around the time and space to unfold. The caterpillar is all about embracing change; if it didn't release the fear of metamorphosis it would never know the thrill of flying.

Animal Keyword:
Caterpillar: Transformation, growth, patience, faith
Owl: Wisdom, protection, authority, awareness, guidance

SIX OF PENTACLES

The Six of Pentacles's story for this deck is one of an assumed symbiotic relationship; however, despite the oxpecker being much smaller in stature, it takes more from the water buffalo than what was initially bargained. The oxpecker uses the water buffalo for the ticks that make their way into the animal's flesh. In return, the birds warn the water buffalo when a predator is near. Seems like a fair trade?

However, the oxpecker doesn't stop with the ticks. The bird also feasts on the water buffalo, picking beyond the tick and feeding on flesh and blood. A little gruesome for sure, but it speaks to that energy of the Six of Pentacles. The power is a bit out of balance. The bird takes advantage of its position enjoying the abundance of resources available through the water buffalo while offering only the bare minimum in return. When you encounter the Six of Pentacles, you may need to consider your position in a situation that calls for one party to be the source of resources and the other the recipient. Are you getting a fair deal? Is the balance of power appropriate, or is one party using their position to an advantage?

If you find that you are asked to make a sacrifice, consider calling on the water buffalo to help you find the situation's wisdom. This firm grounding energy will help you feel connected to the greater good that will result.

Animal Keyword:
Water buffalo: Grounded, honest, patient, reliable
Oxpecker: Bargaining, opportunist

Seven of Pentacles

The spider stepped back to appreciate the work it created during the day. Each web thoughtfully positioned between the branches. It admired the design and examined each one for holes or potential weakness that would allow it prey to escape.

The Seven of Pentacles indicates a time to reflect upon all the work that has led you to this moment in time. It is here that you are asked to examine if you are on the right course for the best results, or do you need to pivot or adjust. Are there any holes or weak spots that would benefit from being filled in?

When you find creating a vision for the future challenging, call upon the spider to guide you through the planning process. The spider brings to your situation patience and a sense of quiet as you connect with your higher self. When you work with the spider's spirit, your "spidey senses" kick in, and you will find the ability to pick up on the vibration that surrounds you and with you will instinctively know the right direction to move.

Animal Keyword:
Spider: Patience, creativity awareness, vibration, connected

EIGHT OF PENTACLES

I may not want to cozy up to a paper wasp's nest, but I can appreciate the workmanship and design that goes into creating one. Could you produce a perfect hexagon from chewed up wood pulp? Me neither! These busy (not bees) can teach us a thing or two about diligence and attention to detail.

When the Eight of Pentacles appears, you may be focused on creating something that keeps you inspired every step of the way. It may be tedious, but the work itself is almost addictive. Your situation may require you to give more than you have in the past; dive in, learn as much as possible, and allow yourself to slip into that ever productive deep state of creative flow. There is but one caveat, and that is you may find yourself lost in perfecting each detail. You may get so caught up or hung up on one small portion of the project that the rest of it never sees the light of day. Use this time to gain as much wisdom and insight as possible—learn from every misstep or miss-cut as it will only help you speed up the process to perfection for future projects. If you are feeling stuck, the Eight of Pentacles may indicate you need outside help or a teacher who can show you the route to success.

The energy of the wasp will keep you inspired to move forward, create, and keep going until the job is done. With the wasp comes a community; when you work with the wasp, you too will find support from those around you who wish to assist you in reaching your goal.

Animal Keyword:
Wasp: Skill, education, mastery, construction, community

NINE OF PENTACLES

The Nine of Pentacles creates an energy that supports some self-care, some relaxation without worrying about all the things on your to-do list, or all the things that could go wrong. It is an energy that keeps that fear of lack area of your brain at bay as you hold off the worry of missing an opportunity while enjoying a much-needed break. When I see this card come up, I know it is time to treat myself. This is not to mean going overboard or spending beyond my means; it is just a permission slip to enjoy a moment of basking in refinement. It's going all out and getting the croissant from the authentic french bakery downtown versus defrosting the mass-produced ones from Costco. Maybe your treat is getting a new haircut from a professional opposed to the kitchen shears (and please, we have all been there...) When you see this card in a reading, ask yourself how you can add a little splurging to the situation to make it all the more enjoyable without taking it to an extreme. If you're focused on a relationship, maybe the Nine of Pentacles is a sign that a date night at a fancy restaurant is in order but resist the urge to empty the bank account for an around the world tour.

If your reading is centered around a career, maybe it's time to splurge on a new outfit that will make you feel more confident in meetings? Sometimes I find the Nine of Pentacles's energy doesn't need to bring anything new into my life but instead creates a comfortable place to just sit on the couch with my kiddo without looking at my phone while merely enjoying her company.The well-fed bear can rest for a season. It is through hibernation that the bear finds renewal.

Call on the bear's strong energy when you need to feel at ease with the pace and rhythm of life. Let it's presence help you feel comfortable enjoying a break or a small indulgence as it will promote rejuvenation. The bear is also one of the animals that comes to us during the night as it guides us through the dream world as we sleep. When you accept the bear's help, you will gain confidence during times of darkness or uncertainty.

Animal Keyword:
Bear: Rest, renewal, guidance, inner-peace

TEN OF PENTACLES

It's time to enjoy the sweet taste of success, but remember that your victory is even more precious when it is shared with others. The Ten of Pentacles asks that you contribute to the greater good and accept that success and good fortune comes with responsibilities. When you use your resources to help others, not only will you strengthen your community, you will build a legacy. How can you apply a long term vision that will have a positive and lasting impact on your current situation? Are you planning ahead with an eye towards a place of permanence? Focusing your efforts on your needs, combined with those of the community, you will lay the foundation for building affluence. When you need to feel part of something bigger, to be a contributing factor to the success of your community or group, use your resources to ensure that the path you created to success does not fill in behind you. Call on the energy of the bee as it will help support you during times of collaboration. When you are in the bee's presence, it is not about the single efforts of one, it is about how the efforts of many work together for a single hive.

Animal Keyword:
Bee: Collaboration, community, prosperity, sweetness of life

PAGE OF PENTACLES

The wise octopus brings to your situation a wealth of assets, from the ability to strategically camouflage itself to regenerating a missing arm. When you call on the octopus' energy, you will feel supportive forces from every angle, creating and generating abundance. The Page of Pentacles brings the message that you have the power to manifest that which you desire, seize the opportunity when it rises. The Page of Pentacles asks that you take purposeful and practical action towards obtaining your goal. Your situation will benefit from a realistic approach, one that places a heavier emphasis on doing rather than dreaming. Your efforts will be rewarded. Stay patient and focused on moving forward. Manifesting a goal can take time, and you may encounter challenges. Use any obstacles or setbacks as a way to prove yourself dependable and dedicated to fully realizing your dream.

When you need to be flexible and adapt to a changing environment quickly, use the octopus' energy to smooth out the transition. This dynamic and intelligent animal creates a healing space after suffering a loss and encourages new growth to emerge as a new strength is formed. When the Page of Pentacles appears to be ready for an opportunity that will spark a change, let the wise octopus help you find clarity in the situation as it propels you forward from the murky water and into an open sea of possibilities.

Animal Keyword:
Octopus: Intelligent, flexible, adaptable, concealing, regrowth

KNIGHT OF PENTACLES

The Knight of Pentacles can be a driving force as this hardworking energy will keep you on track and determined to see a job completed. However, this Knight can also prove to be stubborn, and when out of balance, you may find yourself clinging to an idea or path that is no longer worth pursuing.

When the Knight of Pentacles arrives, you will need to ask yourself if you are embodying the positive traits of the Knight of Pentacles with it's realistic and meticulous approach, or are you being overly-critical and guarded? Are you able to deviate from the plan that has become a source of grief or isn't paying off without feeling as though you have become inconsistent or flakey?

Having perseverance is all well and good when you are working towards a goal that will, in time, be worth the sacrifices made to achieve it, however persistence without the potential for a reward is nothing more than an exercise in futility. For the Knight of Pentacles to be most effective, you need to balance this energy with an element that enjoys fun and relaxation; otherwise, it will be all work and no play, and rarely is that sustainable for too long.

When you encounter the Knight of Pentacles during a reading, you may need to consider if you lack the energy of the Knight and need to buckle down and get to work. On the other hand, if there is an over-abundance of this energy, ask yourself are you clinging to something no longer viable and unable to see your situation differently?

When it comes to letting go of a long-held vision or goal, call on the donkey's energy as it will aid you in finding humility. This determined animal is used for trekking over vast distances, often on narrow rocky paths requiring patience and skill. The donkey will help carry the burden of letting go of something you have held onto for some time, and when you allow this energy in, you will feel a weight lifted from your shoulders. This, in itself, is transformative as you feel lighter and more flexible.

Animal Keyword:
Donkey: Stubborn, balance, agile, strength, determination

QUEEN OF PENTACLES

Long after I created the King and Queen of Pentacles, I discovered the book A Shaman's Guide to Spirit Animals, by Lori Morrison. She lists the cow's keywords as Love, Generosity, and Compassion, and for this royal couple, nothing could be more accurate. When you encounter the Queen of Pentacles, you know it. She is warm, motherly, and generous almost to a fault. If you are in need, she is there ready to support you; however, she can. If you are about to jump on an idea and the Queen of Pentacles arrives, go forward knowing that your resources will not be harmed and, if anything, will grow with her support. The Queen of Pentacles asks that you approach your situation with the same loving energy that she offers to the world. Be generous, be kind, be supportive of those around you, and all that you give will come back in greater abundance. Although wealthy and accustomed to the finer things in life, this is not an energy of garish opulence; no, it is an energy that creates space for all to flourish. When you take on the role of the Queen, not only will you feel like a million bucks, those around you will as well.

The cow brings stable, grounded energy to your situation. This noble and revered animal brings with her the natural energy of a mother, a nurturer, a companion. Call upon the cow's spirit when you need to feel comforted and cared for during times of stress or uncertainty, and she will create around you a loving space for you to thrive.

Animal Keyword:
Cow/Cattle: Grace, nourishment, sacred, guardianship, good fortune, focus

KING OF PENTACLES

When you see the world as a place of abundance with ever-expanding resources, you will feel the King of Pentacles's supportive energy, and you too will be financially free. The King asks that you let go of lack, be generous, release resources because doing so opens the door for new opportunities that will help you generate more wealth. When you focus on lack or feelings of scarcity, you create a block that will prevent abundance or financial gains from freely flowing to you. The King of Pentacles asks that you open your wallet and give what you can without worry or fear. Give the barista at your local coffee shop a little extra, buy a couple of boxes of Girl Scout cookies, donate to your favorite charity—there are plenty of ways to get the positive flow moving. Open the door for positive energy that comes from a generous spirit as it holds power to raise your vibration, and as a result, you will attract more opportunities for wealth and abundance to flow to you.

When you draw the King of Pentacles in a reading, consider if you are stepping in to help a situation, are offering your services and skills to help others succeed or are you holding back?

Because of their eyes' placement, cows have the unique ability to see their position from every angle. Cows/cattle can see what is in front of them and what is behind them; because of this, when you walk with the cow, not only will you gain a vision for the future, you will remember your past. Call on the patient and reliable cow when you need to find perspective—when you feel perhaps detached from your roots, and it will lovingly lead you in the right direction.

Animal Keyword:
Cow/Cattle: Grace, nourishment, sacred, guardianship, good fortune, focus

Quick Reference Guide

The Elements

Fire:

Quality: Hot/Dry

Masculine

Summer

Cards: The Emperor, Strength, Wheel of Fortune,
Temperance, The Tower, Sun, Judgment

Suit of Wands

Positive Attributes:	Negative Attributes:
Adventurous	Aggressive
Creative	Egotistical
Energetic	Impatient
Healthy	Obsessive
Outgoing	Reckless
Risk-taking	Superficial
vibrant	Temperamental

Water:

Quality: Cold/Moist

Feminine

Fall

Cards: The High Priestess, The Chariot, The Hanged-Man, Death, The Moon, Suit of Cups

Positive Attributes:	Negative Attributes:
Calm	Emotional Vampire
Emotional	Fragile
Empathetic	Lazy
Kind	Over-Emotional
Loving	Passive
Patient	Thin-Skinned
Spiritual	Weepy

Air:

Quality: Warm/Moist

Masculine

Spring

Cards: The Fool, The Magician, The Lovers, Justice, The Star

Suit of Swords

Positive Attributes:	Negative Attributes:
Analytical	Blunt
Authoritative	Critical
Clever	Cruel
Direct	Detached
Ethical	Judgmental
Intelligent	Opinionated
Objective	Thoughtless
Witty	

Earth:

Quality: Cold/Dry

Feminine

Winter

Cards: The Empress, The Hierophant, The Hermit,
The Devil, The World,
Suit of Pentacles

Positive Attributes:	Negative Attributes:
Careful	Fearful
Credible	Feeble
Efficient	Gloomy
Factual	Grim
Generous	Nervous
Practical	Stubborn
Proficient	Weak

Thank you Indiegogo Backers!

Amy Jeffreys
Amy Langley
Amy Schimmel
Amy Scott
Amy Wulfing
Amy Yowell
Amyle Hoglin
Andi Miller
Andrea Camburn
Andrea Connell
Andrea Johansson
Andrea Lund
Andrea Thomas
ANDREW CHURCH
Andrew Knox
anette ratama
Angela Buntin
Angela Caccioppo
Angela Hauser
Angela Meyerhoff
Angela White
Angelica Padovani
Angelina Bruno
Angeline Rini
Angie Yingst
Ania Szado
Ann Grens
Ann Hentz
Ann Hupe
Ann Pickl
Ann S Peek
Anna Anderson
Anna Axlund
Anna Bertolet
Anna Joseph
Anna O'Brien-Smith
Anne Chatham Ryan
Anne Cobb
Anne E Lynch
Anne Marie Carter
Anne Reaves
anne tran
anneliese padilla
Annelise Bauer
Annelise d. Strom-Henriksen
Annette Cruz
Annette Gamblin
Annette Stagg
Annie Carrasco
Anthony L.Mehle
Antonia J. Cardella
April Atkins
April FitzGerald
April FitzGerald

April Long
April Nurse
Arianna Siegel
Aricka Harveland
Aricka Harveland
Arraine E Siefert
Arwyn Yarwood
Ashleigh Pippin
Ashley A Westling
Ashley Carroll
Ashley Lapinski
Ashley McElhannon
ashley peterson
Athena Andrzejewski
Athena Mathis
Aubrey E Pervier
Audrea Volker
Audrey DeChadenedes
Augusta Dalziel
Autumn Gonzales
Aya Naganuma
Barbara A. McGavern
Barbara Espinel
Barbara J Wilson
Barbara Jean Yankee
Barbara Kasinski-Moignard
Barbara Knighton
Barbara Kuhn-Center
Barbara O'Dell
Barbe SaintJohn
Bec Gilroy Collins
Becky Filson
Belenda Kemp
Belinda Chambers
Beth Anderson
Beth Anderson
Beth Boatright
Beth Holdridge
Beth Peterson
Bethany Armstrong
Bethany Clark
Bethany Kazimir
Bethany Killian
Bethany Perron
Bett Weston
Blaine Oswald
BOBBI L KINGEN
Bonnie DeLong
Bonnie Kay Webb
Bonnie Keeton
Brandon Riley
Brandy Alyx Reese Giles
Brenda Bass
Brenda Lively

Brenda Quale
Brenda S. Mevorah
Brian R Willis
Brian R Willis
Brian White
Briana Andreoni
Brianna Smith
Bridget Eden
Bridget hardt
Bridget Miller
Bridget Young
Brittany Nelson
Brittany Vance
Bronwen Johnson
Brooke Anna Caine
Bruce Donham
Bruce Reeves
BRUCE W ROBIE
BRUCE W ROBIE
Bryan Kroeger
Bryn Jennings
Caitlin Wagstaff
Caitlin West
Camryn L Indigo
Candace Henry
Candice Craig
Candy Peters
Carla Moffatt
Carol Cubberley
Carol Frail
Carol Gregoire
Carol Hume
Carol Smith
Carole Roesler
Caroline Boyce
Caroline Davies
Caroline Wunn
Carolyn Carter
Carolyn Carter
Carolyn Horn
Carolyn McDermott
Carolynn Warner
Carrie Durlin
Carrie Rich
Caryn Maguire
Cassandra Doeinck
Cassie O'Dell
Cat McKeen
Catherine A. Letteer
Catherine Dodge
Catherine Stine
Cathrine Grundman
Cathy R. Payne
Cathy Raphael

Cathy Raphael
Catrina Rodin
Cecilia Taylor
Celine Zurita
Chantel York
Charita Roberts
Charles Belgarde
Charles Dyer
Chase Johnson
Checka Leinwall
Chenoa Miller
Cherie Aldrich
Cheryl Ashley
Cheryl Ashley
Cheryl Billmyer
Cheryl Cesarini
Cheryl Greenfield
Cheryl L Harrigan
Cheryl Preyer
Chessie Abbott
Chessie Abbott
Chessie Marie Abbott
Cheyl Herries
ChiaYu Cho
Chia-Yu Lin
Chia-Yu Lin
Chloe Brady
Chris fewell
Christa Marro
Christa Marro
Christabel Stuart
Christen Miller
Christin SwÃ¤rdh
Christina MacDonald
Christina Quentin
Christina Ray
Christina Ray
Christine Ashworth
Christine C Bastian
christine cavaliere
Christine Flynn
Christine Hansen
Christine Hauck
Christine Mann
Christine Naber
Christy Hightower
Christy Tashjian
Cindy DeGraw
Cindy Proudfoot
Clare McGlone
Clarence Nikolas
Clarissa Sharp
Clevys J. Monasterios
Codi Stoddard-
Courtright
Colleen M Rauch
Colleen Schumacher

Connie Heap
Connie King
Corinne Loomer
Cortney Mauer
Corvid Freyja
Corvin Greene
COSSONDRA Lynn
MAXEY
Courtney M Privett
Crystal Fisher
Crystal Kocher
Crystal Porch
Cyndi Hedel
cynthia augustyn
Cynthia Baute
Cynthia Byrne
Cynthia Gellis
cynthia Jones
cynthia Jones
Cynthia Jones
Cynthia L Meidinger
Cynthia Taylor
Dacier Iglesias
Dahl-maree Garrigan
Dan Smith
Dana Berry
Dana Dvorak
Dana Flynn
Dana Jenkerson
Dana Miller-Tack
Dana Tate Bailey
Dani Aalfs
Dani Fake
Daniel Colb Rothman
Daniel Connelly
daniel geist
Daniel Hall
daniel keddy
Daniel Miller
Danielle Blair
Danielle Fisher
Danielle Ghasemieh
Danielle Knoll
Danielle Rougeau
Dannaca M Patterson
Daphne Boatright
Darcy Welch
Darlene MacFarland
David Ballard
David Brum
David Gourd
David Iorio Izzo
Davis Sprague
DaVonne Rooney
Dawn Marie Ikehara
Dawn Probst
Dawn Tonneman
deana brandt
Deb Kinney
Deb Novak

Debbi Hartel
Debbie Lake
Debbie Swenson
Deborah L Spathelf
Deborah Bennett
Deborah J. Dunn
Deborah L McManus
Deborah Patterson
Deborah Pitha
Deborah Pontious
deborah sadenwater
Deborrah Trueman
Debra K Little
Deirdre Schwartz
Delilah Howard
Delilah Howard
Dena Warrington
Denise Anderson
Denise Teague
Denise Weinberger
Denver Megel
Derek Schmeh
Derek Schmeh
Desiree Miller
DESOREE BRENNAN
Deva Ludwig
diana boss
Diana Christians
Diana Conces
Diana D'Emeraude
Diana Evers
Diana F Albright
Diane De Bernardo
Diane E Wilson
Diane Volpe
Didier Despois
Dillon C. Harvey
Donald Wellman
Doni Turner
Donna Newton
Dorothy Fitzmorris
Dorothy Fitzmorris
DRUSILLA NICGOWAN
DUBOIS-PICHARD
florence
Dvorah Carrasco
é¦-è¼" ç´€
Echo N Gard
Edda Cain
Eileen Duffy
Eileen Duffy
Eileen Gruber
Elba Sánchez-Short
Elena Polzer
eleni cowsert
Eleni Patrice
Elisa M Cimons
Elisa Townshend
Elisabeth Hansen
Elisabeth Hansen
Elisabeth Schulmeister

Elizabeth Billups
Elizabeth Blakesley
Elizabeth Burns
Elizabeth Daziel
Elizabeth Granda
Elizabeth Grandel
Elizabeth Jaeger
Elizabeth Selk
Elizabeth St Cyr
Elizabeth Stone
Elizabyth Harrington
Ellen Forster
Ellen Mosier
Ellen-Mary O'Brien
Elodie Goodman
Elwanda Leonard
Elyse Kufeldt
Emalee Soddy
Emily Klein
Emily Schuhmann
Emily Schuhmann
Emily Wines
Emmalee Winston
Eric Iverson
Eric Wright
Eric Wright
Erica Holcomb
Erica Keller
Erica Renee Westbrook
Erika Middlebrooks
Erin Bayless
Erin Golden
Erin James c/o QAL
Erin Jones
Erin M LaTurner
Erin MacInnis
Erin Sim
Erin Winters
Erynn Graf
Erynn Graf
Esperanza Richart
Estelle Miller
Eumporn Wood
Eva fernandez
Evelyn Bourne
Evelyn Schumacher
Falon Fowler
Farryn DesBouillons
Farzanah Calis
felicia fowler
Felicia Murray
Fiona Kelly
Fiona Kelly
FRAN SMITH
Francesca P. Simonelli
Gae Weber
Gail Morse
Gale Hamby
Garth Tardy
Gayle Helps
Gayle Thorley

Geary Johns
George tsouroudiakakis
Geralyn Hughes
Geralyn Hughes
Gigi DiBlasio
Gilliauna Davis
GINA GILLS
Gina McKenzie
Gina Millar
Ginger Stevens
Giuliani Askland
Glenda Dianne Walker
Grace Holt
Grace M. Looney
Greg Skrtic
Gregory A Churchill
Gretchen Demmin
Gretchen Nutt
Gretchen Parker
Gwyn McVay
Hanako Fukunaga
Hannah McInnis
Hannah Pyne
Hannes Beecken
Heather Anderson
Heather Carroll
Heather Hutchison
Heather Lynn Roundtree
Heather Turner
Heather Vandegrift
Heather Wagner
Heidi Cruz
Heidi Geis
Heidi Phillips
Helen Bourne Schmid
Helen Gerth Mahi
Helen Windsor
Helga Conklin
Hettienne Grobler
Hilary B. Mohr
Hillary Adams
Hillary Feldmeyer
Hillary Feldmeyer
Hillary Norris
Holli Harper
Hollie Glenn
Holly Griwach
Holly Myers
Holly Myers
Holly Westbrook
Howard Wright
Ian Lovecraft
Ida Umphers
Ila Brook Markley
InÄ's Vollmer
Inger Anne-Sofi
OrtenlÄ¶f
Ingrid Emilsson
Ingrid Norsic
Ingrid O'Neill
Irina Klimenko

J Reale
Jacquie Evans
Jadwiga McKay
Jaia Konik
Jaila Hansen
Jaime P Kelly
Jaime Thompson
james isaac
James Juliani
Jami McMillan
JAMIE L WALLACE
Jamie Ledford
Jamie Scripps
Jan Edmondson
Jane Phillips
Janette Smith
Janice Chao
Janice Hildebrand
Janice King
Janice RossJ
Janie Felix
Jann McKenzie
Jann Selleck
Jasmine Jaffarian
Jasmine Seka Williams
Jason pfleegor
Jayne Brewer
Jean Rowe
Jeanine Southall
Jeanmarie White
Jeanne Dunn
Jeanne Dunn
Jeannette Cranford
Jeannie Leighton
Jeffrey Ballam
Jeffrey Tyler
Jen Brown
Jen Moraga
Jen Sankey
Jeneva Mobley
JENIFER STROUD
Jennie King
Jennifer A Reece
Jennifer Ball
Jennifer Beaman
Jennifer Bland
Jennifer Bledsoe
Jennifer Branscumb
Jennifer Campbell
Jennifer Capone
Jennifer Chartrand
Jennifer Eagan
Jennifer Fay
Jennifer Feuchter
Jennifer Forness
Jennifer Frandsen
Jennifer H Jewett
Jennifer Jones-galyean
Jennifer King
Jennifer Molina
Jennifer O'Brennan
Jennifer Parsons

Jennifer Pearson
Jennifer Provencher-Neuberg
Jennifer Rushforth
Jennifer Sumi
Jennifer Tarver
Jennifer Watkins
Jennifer West
Jennifer White
Jennifer White
Jennifer Wilson
Jennifer Winn
Jenny Morris
Jesamyn Angelica
Jess Brown
Jessica Barabe
Jessica Francq
Jessica Gray
Jessica Hamilton
Jessica Holloway
Jessica Kanzig
jessica l zakowski
Jessica MacMillan
Jessica Miles
Jessica Miles
Jessica Smith
Jessica Snow White
Jessie Driscoll
Jey Parks
Jhaden Lanfield
Jill Martin
Jill Morris
Jill Morris
Jill Salmon
Jill Stolinas
Jillian A Robbins
Jillian Schnalzer
Jim Spanks
Jo Lister
Joan Anne Dougherty
Joan Connorton
Joan Connorton
Joan Crowley
Joan Gaetz
JoAnne Drake
JoAnne Remillard
Jodi DeAngelis
Jodi Maas
Jody Harrison
Jody Johnson
Joey Salcido
Johanna Kubicek
John Korianitis
John Michael Gallagher jr
Jolene Long
Jordan Lagana
Joseph Benitez
Josh Vanden Busch
Joshua Pool
Joya Parsons
Judith Illes

Judith Jurgaitis
Judy Noll
Juli Beighley
Julia Gordon-Bramer
Julianne Victoria
Julie Cox
Julie Grigor
Julie Klumb
Julie Knoecklein
Julie Mattson
Kae Elmquist
Kaile Dutton
Kailey Rose Campbell
Kara Bryant
Kara Webber
Karen Auger
Karen Bankert
Karen Copestakes
KAREN HENDRICKX
Karen Soloff
Karen Townsend
Kari Giles
Kari Naperstak
Karie Schroder
Karin Levitski
Karin Rölsarne
Karl Schmidt
Karly Latham
Kat Kremske
Kat Yrizarry
Kate Heiber-Cobb
Kate sill
Kate Silveira
Kate Toye
Katelyn Gehringer
Katharine Elizabeth Sullivan
Katharine Houk
Katherin Sloan
Katherine Curran
Katherine Hayford
Katherine Rowe
Katherine Vondy
Kathleen Buffone Dassier
Kathleen J. Kaminski
Kathleen Little
Kathryn Coll
Kathryn Gorman-Lovelady
Kathryn St Clare
Kathy Rudzena
Kathyrn Myers
Katie Andersson
Katie Andersson
Katie Sweeney
Katrina Clay
Katy Hoffer
Katy Kingston
Katya Batlle
Kayleigh Hopkins
Kelli Laws
Kellie Sexton

Kelly Briley
Kelly Davidian
Kelly Davidian
Kelly Fitzgerald
Kelly Kurttila
Kelly Natalie Davis
Kelly Olson
Kelly Sroka
Kelsea Habecker
Kendra Bailey
kenneth eastman
kenneth eastman
Kenneth W Bowlby
Keri Alley
kerri snook
Kerry Houston
Kerstein Finan
Ketura Wisner
Keyly Garrison
Keyly Garrison
Kim Betros
Kim Fuller
Kim Heil
Kim Heil
Kim Laven
Kim Maxwell
Kim McGillivray
Kim Schmitt
Kimberley Ellis
Kimberley Lutz
Kimberly Curington
Kimberly Fordham
Kimberly Jones
Kimberly Lorraine Daugherty
Kimberly Mendoza
Kirk Olsen
Korina Kaffka
Kris Haskell
Kris Korz
Kris Mancuso
Kristen Koenig
Kristen McKinlay
Kristen Wallace
Kristi Huffman-Green
Kristie Sarson
Kristie Sarson
Kristin Holt
Kristin McCollough
Kristina Gordon
Kristina Sturdivant
Kristine Balog
Kristine Bolstridge
Kristine Kazel
Kristine Schend
Kristy Tackett
Krysta Brinkley
Krystal Henderson
Kuah Sing Yee
Kyle McKenzie

Kylie Logan
Lacey Stewart
Lacie Sorensen
Lani Glanville
Lara Whelan
Laraine Herring
Laura Cohen
Laura Counsel
Laura Gisseman
Laura Jones
Laura Laubach-Richardson
Laura Lindsay
Laura Mailloux
Laura Mesick
Laura Rider
Laura Schappert
Laura Strowman
Laura Strowman
Laura Williams
Laura Wooster
Laurelle Martin
Lauren Butner
Lauren Olson
Lauren OLSON
Laurie A Silver
Laurie Claxton
Laurie Smith
Laurie Stephens
LeAnn Cramer
Lee Ann Wasson
Lee Taylor
Lee Wood
Lennika Wright
Leon Jia Hui
Leslie Harris
Leslie Jubilee
Leslie Weaver
Liadan Ryland
Liao, An-Ting å»-æ^©é¼Ž
Lihsett Padro
Linda B Sealey
Linda Bean
Linda Bock
Linda Cota
Linda Evenson
Linda Fox
Linda Johnson
Linda Jordan-Eichner
Linda Perkins
Lindsay Schroeder
Lindsay Sheldon
Lindsey Tzikakos
Lindsey Winot
Lisa Anderson
Lisa Anderson
Lisa Bain
Lisa Belles
Lisa Casella
Lisa Daughters
lisa dee port white
Lisa Dobry
Lisa Hibbard
Lisa Hughes

Lisa J. Wolper
Lisa Jones
LISA LIPINSKI
Lisa Luna Turnpaugh
Lisa Marie Sage
Lisa Martinez
Lisa Piver
Lisa R Barry
Lisa R McNany
Lisa Rocklin
Lisa Schoenfeld
Lisa Sciamanda
Lisa Turnpaugh
Lisa Waldron
Lisa Weikel
Lise Pacioretty
Liz Trotman
Liz Westwater
Liz Pfeiffer
Lora Vencill
Lori Banks
Lori Bridge
Lori Fox
Lori Gottschalk
Lori Larocque
Lori Nielsen
lori rollins
Louise Posch
Luba Richards
Luci Sweet
Luz Lucia
Lynda G Gordon
Lynda Schumacher
Lynette Brown
Lynn Genevieve
Lynn Rollins
Lynn Zukowski
Lynna Landstreet
Lynne Denise Harrell
Lynne Harrell
Lynne Princigalli
Lynne Tyson
M Riley
MÃ©lanie Richer
Madelene Antrim
Madelyn Pitts
Madelyn Pitts
Madison Bankston
Mae S Salinsky
Magda Pecsenye
Maida Combs
Maija Salins
Mairead O'Sullivan Leong
Maleena Tickle
Malley Heinlein
Manuela Lima
Marc B
Marci Frey
Marcie Lynn Wason
Marcy Leng
Margaret Fivash
Margaret Fulton
Margaret Quigley

Marguerite R Hutton
Maria Biniasz
Maria Holland
Marie Miller
Marie White
Marije Westerhof
Mariko Shewmake
Marinca Kaldeway
MARION KROTT
MARION KROTT
Marisa Mirviss
Mark Best
Markie Burnhope
Marne Oyen
Marsha Hostetler
Martha c Pease
Martha Klingler
Martine de Ridder
Mary Lee Agnew
Mary Ann Frank
Mary Ann Donnarumma
Mary Ann Kae
Mary Ann Kae
Mary Barzee
Mary Beth Holtz
Mary Brandner
Mary Krajnovich
Mary L. Poe
Mary Lynne Biener
Mary Malone
Mary Mannix
Mary murphy
Mary T Cusack
MaryAnna Clemons
Marybeth Roden
Matthew Chase
Matthew Dombroski
Matthew Self
Maura J Newell
Maureen Betita
Maureen kane
Maureen L Thomas
Maureen Willigan
Maxia Kaough
MAYU WATANABE
Medora Van Denburgh
Meg Wittenmyer
Megan Long
Megan Metcalf
Megan Rollo
Megan Sirr
Megan Springate
Megan Warner
Meghan Hakala
Meghan Medici
Megin Brooks
Melanie Grenier-Brusse
Melanie Oborne
Melanie Widmer
Melisa Mitchell
Melissa Berger
Melissa Dawn McCoy

Melissa Garrett
Melissa Gigliotti
Melissa Hamilton
Melissa Loomer
Melissa Mortensen
Melissa Raso
Melissa Rivera
Melissa Scavetta
Melissa Selvaggio
Melissa Skillings
Melissa Tuggle Ward
Melissa Wilson
Melody Huckins
Memarie Livingood
Meredith Renduchintala
Merri Anne Stowe
Mia Dean
Michael Adam Smedley
Michael Ferrantino
Michael Forman
Michael Green
Michael Green
Michele Graves
Michele Tyler-Walters
Michele Tyler-Walters
Michelle Braun
Michelle Burgess
Michelle Catlett
Michelle Crawford-Bewley
Michelle D Gouin
Michelle Grunden
Michelle Ho
Michelle Kennedy
Michelle Martel
Michelle Robinson
Michelle Seamons
Mika Arai
Mika Potter
Milyn King
Mina Edgerton
mindy brady
Miranda Cordova
Mitchell Woloschek
Molly Sexton
Molly Sumridge
Monica Garcia
Monica Greaney
Monica Haltvik
Monica McCormick
monica nelson
Monica Salvi
Monika Grabiec
Monika salden
Monte Burns
Monte Burns
Morgan Peckol
MORGAN STEBBINS
Mrs Joy Henderson
Mrs Joy Henderson
Mynde Mayfield
Myrna Darlene Taylor
Myrna Martin

N Sage Cara
Nadine Schmidt
Nadine Spates
Nancy A Pietrzykowski
Nancy Benham
Nancy Bryant
Nancy Gear
Nancy Hendrickson
Nancy L Johnson
Nancy M. Doucette
Nancy Oberg
Nancy Ruel
Naoko Taniguchi
Naomi Rabinowitz
Natalie E Anderson
Natalie Gupton
Natalie Peterson
Natasha Lucana-Godfrey
Natasha Parvin
Natasha Parvin
Nedre Carter
Nicholas Cendese
Nicholas Ong
Nicholas Ong
Nichole Alex
Nichole Groft
Nicole Christ
Nicole Collantes Marnet
Nicole Dipaulo
Nicole Foos
Nicole McCumber
Nicole Nunes
Nicole Petronzio
Nicole Sorrentino
Nicole Tihlarik
Nicole Wtork
Nicole Yaeger
Niki Blomqvist
Nina Kohl
Noelle Nicholls
Noelle-Lynn Peregrino
Nora Hendrickson
Noreen A Thompson
NormaAlicia Pino
Novella Gutierrez
Nyrel cederstrom
Odeth Aranda
Oilda Villanueva
Olivia Gross
Paige Diner
Paige Downing
Pam Bzoch
Pam Turlow
Pamela B Tiger
Pamela Carter
Pamela January
Pamela Kirschbaum
Pamela Kohlman
Pamela Patterson
Pamela Patterson
Pamm Horbit

Pat House
Patience Harvey
Patricia
Patricia Acquaire
Patricia Brown
Patricia Harrigan
Patricia Lacy
Patricia Lay
Patricia Lemieux
Patricia Rivers
Patricia S. Gormley
Patryce Eleazer
Patty Combs-Bialik
Paula Bischoff
Paula Bubacz
PeiSyuan He(ä½•ä½©ç'‡)
PF Anderson
PF Anderson
Phoenix Hilson
PK HARLING-CHALLIS
Polly Felton
Priscilla Barrett
Priscilla Marden
rachael harrod
Rachael Hatefi
Rachael Omps
Racheal Martin
Rachel Avery
Rachel Briggs
Rachel galbreath
Rachel Hutcheson
rachel romo
Rachel tookes
Rachel Wargofcak
Rachel Yukimura
Rachelle Verges
rae bain
Randi Johnson
Randi Miller-Grasseth
Randy Elliott
Raydeen Graffam
Rebecca Douglas
rebecca fox
Rebecca Hullenbaugh
rebecca jenks
Rebecca Johnson
Rebecca L. Wood
Rebecca MacNaughton
Rebecca Martin
Rebecca McDonald
Rebecca Meyer
Rebecca Ross
Rebecca Saywell
Rebecca Sprauer
Rebecca Thomas
Rebecca Yaeger
Rebeccah Kocak
Rebekah Britton
Rebekah Stephens
Rebekah Sweet
Reese Clapp

Renee Demaray
Renee M Valois
Renee Smith
Rob Potter
Robert Alvarez
Robert Russell
Roberta Schrang
Roberta Vibbert
Robin Dolan
Robin Eubanks
Rodney Hartman
Ron Simpson
Ronda Kisner
Rosa Marques
Rosa Moudene
Rosalind Laraway
Rose Fewtrell
rose garlo
Rose Rathbun
Rose Thiessen
Roseanne K Curtis
Rosemary Wright
Rosie Kae
Roxane Stoner
Roxanne Cargill
Roxanne Harrison
Roxanne Harrison
Russell LaFazia
Ruth Hagen
Ruth Clark
Ruth Marie Fledermaus
Ruth Renate Davidson
Ryan Angel
Ryan Huser
Ryan Rudy-Logue
Sabrina Caldwell
Sachi Thornley
Saivite Wilson
Sally Griffith
Sally Palmer
Sally Sprowl
Samantha Cowan
Samantha Ehrman
Samantha Grodecki
Samantha Groom
Samantha Johnson
Samantha Wright
Sandra Clare
Sandra Evette
Sandra Evette
Sandra Jackson
Sandra Lynne Claar
Sandra Quenon
Sandra Seery
Sara Brinson
Sara Lipowitz
Sara Strommer Sara Wyen
Sarah Joyce
Sarah B Fenton
Sarah Baird
Sarah Boshart
Sarah Bruckler

Sarah Bumstead
Sarah Clark
Sarah Drabert
Sarah Duncan
Sarah E Kahn
Sarah Gilleland
Sarah Langner
Sarah Makarechian
Sarah Newman
Sarah Nimmo
Sari K. Wolf
Sarrah Young
Savannah Spencer
Scott Hyjek
Shaela Cook
Shalimar M Shumway
Shana Moorefield
Shannon Bostwick
Shannon Bradbury
Shannon Christopher
Shannon J Arnold
Shannon McCabe
Shannon Murray
Shannon Williams
Shannon Wilson
Shara Pangburn
Sharia Des Jardins
Sharon Pogodzinski
Sharon A Wilson
Sharon Barbour
Sharon Jackson
Sharon Martens
Sharon Martens
Sharon Tiahrt
Sharon Wells
Shauna Rose
Shawn Stendevad
Shawn Stendevad
Shawn Telkamp
Sheehan Rosen
Sheila Kargel
Sheila Koenig
Sheila Olszewski
Sheila Winegarden
Shelbi Good
Shelby Corring
Shelley Carter
Shelley Smith
Shereen Rayle
Sheri Nugent
Sheri Nugent
Sherrie H. Sinclair
Sherrie L Dillon
Sherry Farley
Sherry Havercamp
Sherry McCutcheon
Sherry Railsback
Shilo Orellana
Shiri Sondheimer
Shyla Christin
SIN SORACCO
Siobhan McLeod
Skylar Perry

SO WAI PIU RAYMOND	Susan Royal	Tina R Parsons	YUKA TSUJIMOTO
Sofia Tascon	Susan Ruhl	Tineke Naseef	Yuko Suga
Sol Olid	Susan Sandenaw	Ting Hao, Yang	Yvette Hewitt
Sophia Schlegelmilch	Susan Shedd	Tobias Kennedy	Yvonne Colley
Stacey Averkieff	Susan W Gould	Toby C Levens	Yvonne Loveday
Stacey Greenberg	Susan Watts	Tom G Furtwangler	Zachary Robinson
Stacey Hankins	Susie Tarman	Tommie Gillam	Zeratha M Young
Stacey witt	Susyn Klein	Tommy Dingus	ZoÃ« Marchani
staci l. smith	Suzanne DeHaven	Tonya Craft	Zoe Pollock
Stacy Southwell	Suzanne Kash	Tory Gough	
Stacy Bressette	Suzanne Livingston	Tracey Ledel	
Stacy Garwood	Suzanne Moore-Ullrich	Tracy Hopler	
Stacy Johnson	Suzanne Stewart	Tracy Lauman	
Stacy L Henson	Suzanne Windsor	Tracy Smith	
Stacy L Inness	Sylvia Frazier	Trish Sullivan	
Stacy Robello	Tahnee Kneeland	Trixy Reed	
Stacy Weidmann	Tamara Allredge	Troy Davis	
Star Bustamonte	Tamara Blyden	Trucia Quistarc	
Stefanie Harper	Tamara Brody	Trudy Hingley	
Steph Thomas	Tamara E. Davis	Tsz Fung Yue	
Stephanie Alvarez	Tamara E. Davis	Valerie Cates	
Stephanie Asher	Tamara Ishmael	Valerie Kemp	
Stephanie Baldridge	tamara silva	Valerie Schiavone	
Stephanie Carter	Tammi Altenburger	Valerie Sonnenthal	
Stephanie Chesson	Tammy Dunn	Valerie Sylvester	
stephanie Davis	Tammy M Batley	Valor Grimm	
Stephanie Gladden	Tammy Warden	Vanessa Bernstein	
Stephanie Heitman	Tamora Vang	Vanessa Glass	
Stephanie Jacobs	Tamsyn Cave	vanessa ronsse	
Stephanie Kays	Tanin Powers	Velma E Renney	
Stephanie L Spitzer	Tanya Dunn	Veronica Salvati	
Stephanie mason	Tara Leduc	Vicki Brown	
Stephanie Oaks	Tatyana young	Vickie Trancho	
Stephanie Romero	Taylor Stretch	Vicky Herrick	
Stephanie Saible	Taylor Wile	Vicky L Hall	
Stephanie Spencer	Teresa Knezek	Victoria Bennett	
Stephanie Spencer	Teresa Lai	Victoria HOBAN READ	
Stephanie Stewart	Teresa Samuel	Victoria McNally	
Stephanie Sullivan	Teresa Woods	Victoria Turner	
Stephanie Vannoy	Terra Breemes	Victoria Yee	
Stephanie Williams	Terri Emler	Vinita Chhugani	
Stepheny Isbell	Terri Hackler	Virginia McFadin	
Steve hooper	Terri Lynn McNichol	Vladlena Costescu	
Steve Parker	Terri Maddox	Vonn Scott Bair	
Sue Billings	Terri Simon	Wai Yim	
Sue Chapman	Terri Yeomans	Wanda Olszewski	
Sue Landsman	Terri-Lynn McNichol	Wendy Conger	
Sue Wilkinson	Terry Bussard	Wendy Fisher	
Sunyoung Park	Terry L McGhee Jr	Wendy Gormly-Kester	
Susan Davidson	Theresa Ottosen	Wendy Jie	
Susan Herbst	Therese Porter	wendy mcgowen	
Susan Lang	Thesanica Chan	Wendy Seigman	
Susan Leksche	Thora M Caillech	Wendy Space	
Susan Loblaw	Tiffany Fox	Wendy Williamson	
Susan Mahlburg	Tiffany Harrison	Wendy Wise	
Susan Mahlburg	Tiffany Zaremba	Willow Moon	
Susan McCuistion	Tika Viteri	Yasmine Galenorn	
Susan Montrose	Timothy Robbins	Yeda Perry	
Susan Powell	Tina Bystrom	Yoo Coolness	
Susan Robinson	Tina Forsyth	Yoshimi Pelc	
Susan Rossi	Tina Kim Vaccarello		

Made in the USA
Columbia, SC
28 October 2020